DEEPEST DIFFERENCES

A Christian-Atheist Dialogue

JAMES W. SIRE AND CARL PERAINO

IVP Books

An imprint of InterVarsity Press
Downers Grove, Illinois

InterVarsity Press
P.O. Box 1400, Downers Grove, IL 60515-1426
World Wide Web: www.ivpress.com
Email: email@ivpress.com

InterVarsity Press® *is the book-publishing division of InterVarsity Christian Fellowship/USA*®*, a movement of students and faculty active on campus at hundreds of universities, colleges and schools of nursing in the United States of America, and a member movement of the International Fellowship of Evangelical Students. For information about local and regional activities, write Public Relations Dept., InterVarsity Christian Fellowship/USA, 6400 Schroeder Rd., P.O. Box 7895, Madison, WI 53707-7895, or visit the IVCF website at <www.intervarsity.org>.*

Scripture quotations, unless otherwise noted, are from the New Revised Standard Version of the Bible, *copyright 1989 by the Division of Christian Education of the National Council of the Churches of Christ in the USA. Used by permission. All rights reserved.*

Design: Cindy Kiple

ISBN 978-0-8308-3358-0

Printed in the United States of America ∞

Library of Congress Cataloging-in-Publication Data

Sire, James W.
 Deepest differences: a Christian-atheist dialogue / James W. Sire and Carl Peraino.
  p. cm.
 Includes bibliographical references and index.
 ISBN 978-0-8308-3358-0 (pbk.: alk. paper)
 1. Christianity and atheism. I. Peraino, Carl. II. Title.
 BR128.A8S57 2008
 261.2'1—dc22

                                                                                                        2008046024

P 25 24 23 22 21 20 19 18 17 16 15 14 13 12 11 10 9 8 7 6 5 4 3 2 1

Y 30 29 28 27 26 25 24 23 22 21 20 19 18 17 16 15 14 13 12 11 10 09

Contents

Acknowledgments

We, the authors, would like to acknowledge the friendship and occasional counsel of Phil Matejczyk, who heard much of this dialogue secondhand as each of us kept him apprised of at least some of our discussion. Our wives, Nancy and Marj, were patient with us, listening to our off-computer expostulations of surprise and, sometimes, frustration. Marj, who has long saved Jim from terrible typos, proofread the manuscript at an early stage. Thanks are also due to our editor, Jim Hoover, and his colleagues.

Finally, Jim thanks God for giving him a long life with and a mind fascinated by the mysteries of God and his universe. Carl feels fortunate that he emerged into sentience in a relatively benign environment via the concatenation of innumerable chance events spanning millions of years of evolution.

Preface

Deepest Differences is the brainchild of Jim Sire and Carl Peraino, two retired guys who met at a neighborhood book club.[1] Soon they became aware they were committed to worldviews that were radically at odds. Carl had been an atheist from the early days of college, Jim a committed Christian (Carl might say a Christian who should be committed) since seventh grade. However they came to their different understandings of reality, they certainly had thought about them long and hard.

The book club had been a congenial place to meet, find out about each other's interests and build mutual respect. Given the specific material nature of the universe, Carl would say, the email dialogue that constitutes this book was inevitable. Jim would say that, though it was not inevitable, it had been in the mind of God from before the foundation of the world. And there it is—the heart of their different worldviews—displayed oddly and cryptically but, when these views are elaborated, both obviously and well.

With Jim and Carl, what was on the verge of happening needed something to get it going. That catalyst occurred at a quiet lunch at the Morton Arboretum where Jim and his wife, Marj, by coincidence met Carl and Phil, another member of the book club.

It was Jim's penchant for light-hearted needling that provided the spark. He had just read the obituary of Kurt Vonnegut, an author many of whose black-humored novels Jim had long ago devoured. He suggested that Vonnegut had, perhaps unwittingly, given an argument for the existence of

---

[1] Although independently generated, this work complements and extends an earlier, similarly structured dialogue between Drs. Preston Jones and Greg Graffin. See "Relevant Readings."

God. Carl protested. Jim rejoined. Some eighty emails later, both had been surprised and frustrated with the recalcitrance of the other. Neither had changed his mind. Each thought that at least some of his own arguments were good. So why did they not persuade?

Their closing essays in the book attempt to answer this question, but astute readers will be able to write their own final chapter to the book.

Some readers, Jim thinks, will be persuaded to change their minds; reason and the Spirit of God will have done their work. Carl will say that every change of mind, and there may be some, simply illustrates the causal nexus of the universe doing its thing.

Well, let human reason, the Spirit of God and the causal nexus of the universe begin doing their thing (or is it things?).

Jim Sire
Carl Peraino

Editorial Note

First, the exact sequence of emails has not been strictly followed. Rather, the order has been arranged to capture the flow of the argument; to this end, emails covering the same main topic have been put in logical sequence. What has been strictly preserved is both the intellectual content and the verbal form. This is realistic dialogue in the raw, with emotions pitching up and down as one or the other of them has struck a nerve or stimulated surprise.

Second, the subject headings have been changed to indicate more accurately the content of each main entry, and subheads have been added to clarify the course of the argument.

Third, footnotes, a list of relevant readings and a study guide have been added for clarification and reference to further perspective on the topic at hand.

Finally, a subject index has been added to aid those interested in easily accessing all the comments on a particular topic—intelligent design or morality, for example.

PART ONE

SLIPPING INTO DIALOGUE

The dialogue that constitutes this book began with Jim's casual comment about Amadeus Mozart and Kurt Vonnegut. Two friends who knew they disagreed about lots of things—God, human beings and the universe— exchanged innocent banter. After the first email response, however, the substance of discourse gradually began to focus and then to fan out.

1

Mozart, Bach and Vonnegut   Signals of Transcendence

Dear Carl and Phil:

You may remember the sidebar in yesterday's Arboretum conversation: A discussion about "life without Mozart" being like a desert strewn with rusting beer cans.[1]

I mentioned an argument from aesthetic experience made by Catholic philosophers Peter Kreeft and Ron Tacelli (of Boston College):

> There is the music of Johann Sebastian Bach.
> Therefore there must be a God.
> You either see this one or you don't.[2]

Then I commented on the fact that I had just recently heard this argument, but couldn't remember who said it. Well, it was Kurt Vonnegut, who just died at eighty-four.

In a speech to students at the University of Wisconsin, "Knowing What's Nice," Vonnegut said this:

> My epitaph, should I ever need one, God forbid: "The only proof he ever needed for the existence of God was music."[3]

Vonnegut, of course, was being no more literal with this remark than he was with 90 percent of every remark he ever made or ever wrote. It still shows, however, how close he was to recognizing a *signal of transcendence* (Peter Berger's term), that is, a signal that there is in or behind the universe something, perhaps

---

[1] Jim and Carl, Jim's wife and another friend, Phil, had unexpectedly met and lunched together at the Morton Arboretum in Lisle, Illinois.

[2] Peter Kreeft and Ronald K. Tacelli, *Handbook of Christian Apologetics* (Downers Grove, Ill.: InterVarsity Press, 1994), p. 81.

[3] Quoted on PBS's *The News Hour*.

even a personal something, that is not to be reduced to material reality—no matter how wave-like or particle-like matter is. One could say that Vonnegut was close (that is, close but no cigar) to moving from an atheism bordering on nihilism to an agnosticism bordering on belief. In the final analysis, despite his attempt at being what he called a Humanist, his nihilism really won out.

Here's how he closes "Knowing What's Nice":

> What about God, if He were alive today? Gil Berman [one of Vonnegut's fictional characters] says, "God would have to be an Atheist, because the excrement has hit the air-conditioning big time, big time."[4]

Jim Sire

2

Signals Disallowed

Phil, a long-time friend of both Carl and Jim, sometimes read and commented on the ensuing emails. It was Carl, however, who quickly realized he was being challenged. So he is the one who replied.

Dear Jim:

Thanks for sending the Vonnegut speech; I really enjoyed it.

If you are implying that a faint "signal of transcendence" was reaching Kurt, I would strongly disagree. I think he would roll around on the floor, laughing at such a suggestion. Moreover, I think you mischaracterize him as a nihilist. I see

---

[4] You can access his irreverent, obscene, very funny Wisconsin speech at <www.vonnegutweb.com/archives/arc_nice.html>. Or try searching for "Knowing What's Nice" on the Internet.

him as a profoundly moral secular humanist with a great gift of satire, which he used to great effect against the hypocrisies of our "faith-based" society.

Evidently I'm unworthy because I'm not getting any signal from the "something," personal or not, beyond and above the material universe. If this "something" is out there, it and all the souls of the faithfully departed surely must be in torment about the way things are going here on earth. That would kind of rob the afterlife of the eternal orgasm of happiness that everyone seems to anticipate. Of course, in the realm of the transcendent there could be total insulation from the material world so all inhabitants of that realm would be oblivious to the agonies suffered by their descendants, relatives, friends or just earthlings in general. Is that what believers hope for?

Hey, what about dem Bears?[5]

Carl

3

Vonnegut   Humanist or Nihilist

Dear Carl:

Yes, I imagine that Vonnegut would roll around on the floor laughing, if he were still living, of course. From his present position, who knows? I'll not speculate. Still, he did love music, and there was the sign. He saw it and in death's-head humor turned it into a joke.

---

[5] "What about dem Bears?" is a phrase Jim would use to change the subject when he was tired of the way a conversation was going. Carl uses it to tease Jim about his possible annoyance at his remarks.

Vonnegut— humanist or nihilist? I also agree that he would call himself a humanist and that, as you say, as a moralist and satirist he took on "the hypocrisies of our 'faith-based' society." As a humanist, he also took on a number of other issues—war, for example. It is not his moralism that is under question—only his lack of a basis for it. Without some sort of transcendent foundation for morality, morality can only be whatever people think it should be. Vonnegut is no more an authority on this than Hitler. Both thought that the practice of their moral views would improve the world. Without something outside the system of human imagination and desire, no one has any right to claim that their system is better than anyone else's. We should chat about this sometime.

There is an irony here. As a complete and utter materialist (i.e., one who believes that matter/energy is all there is), he too is part of a "faith-based society." His materialism is every bit as based on faith as is a Christian or any other person who believes in God. It might take me some time to lay out the case for this, but suffice it to say that materialism is not self-evident. Even the so-called self-evident truth of the law of noncontradiction resides on the assumption that the consciousness that recognizes the law (and the necessity for its truth) is not itself asleep. Can you prove to yourself—I mean really prove without a shadow of a doubt—that you are awake as you read this email? Materialism requires much more faith. I don't mean that there is no good argument for it, just that it can never be such a telling argument that one cannot find some reason to doubt it or to undermine the argument for it. So for Vonnegut to rail against a "faith-based society" is to rail against his own railing.

Transcendence as immanence Transcendence does not necessarily eliminate the simultaneous omnipresence of the transcendent. That may sound like gobbledygook, but what I am trying to say is that a being that is transcendent can also be present. Christian theology, for example, speaks of God as both transcendent and immanent. The Other is with us. The transcendent is also immanent. If God really did create the universe in the sense that once there was no material reality and now there is, surely he is present to it. It has no existence except the one he gives it; if he goes away, stops sustaining existence, it goes away.

Those like me (and that's most of the world, whether Christian or not) occasionally recognize signals of transcendence, little glimpses into a world beyond. One of those signals is *music*. Even rap displays order and design. But then there is Bach and Handel and Brubeck.

I will leave to later my comments on the problem of evil and suffering. It's not necessarily tied to the notion of signals of transcendence.

Jim

4

Almost Human, and Sometimes Smarter

Between the previous and the following email, Carl sent Jim the web link to "Almost Human, and Sometimes Smarter" by John Noble Wilford, published in the New York Times *in April 2007.[6] This article summarized observations by several scientists, including Jane Goodall, Andrew Whiten and Richard Wrangham, who noted the "remarkable range of behavior and talent" of chimps. Wilford does not explicitly liken any of this behavior to morality, but Jim assumed that the reason Carl referred him to it meant that Carl was offering an alternative and completely naturalistic explanation of human morality.*

---

[6]John Noble Wilford, "Almost Human, and Sometimes Smarter," *New York Times,* April 17, 2007, F2.

Genes and morality

Dear Carl:

There may well be a genetic dimension to animal behavior that appears to echo ethical behavior in humans. There may be as well a genetic dimension to the human embodiment of moral motions.[7] Perhaps that's an aspect of the mechanism that God designed in both. Perhaps there is a merely animal base from which human beings came via some sort of biological evolution. But there are two issues that the biological aspect of humans does not really address.

First, human beings could have evolved from an ancestor common to both apes and them. The issue is not evolution but nondirected evolution, that is, whether the appearance of human beings is explained by some sort of Darwinian or neo-Darwinian totally naturalistic mechanism, a mechanism not under the control or auspices of the divine. Scientists like Richard Dawkins think there is such a mechanism and that its existence has been demonstrated by science. Scientists like Francis Collins do not think so; human DNA is rather, in some nonnaturalistic sense, the "language of God."

Moral behavior and moral principle

Second, as human beings we believe—or if we don't believe, we act as if we believe—that there is a genuine distinction between what is and what ought to be. Beating children till they bleed and die is absolutely wrong, not because all but a very few people believe it is wrong, but because it really is wrong. So likewise is the massacre of thirty-two students and faculty.[8] We display the fact that we think such acts are absolutely wrong all the time. But if nature is all there is, then there is no difference between right and wrong. There are only opinions.

---

[7] *Moral motions* include both the particular notions of right and wrong and the human disposition to act according to these notions.

[8] The killings at Virginia Polytechnic Institute and State University on April 16, 2007, occurred just before this email was written.

Moral motions must be grounded in something outside the material world order. Theists, for example, say that the moral motions displayed by human beings are grounded in Godlikeness; something is moral because it expresses or imitates the character of God as good, i.e., utterly righteous. Righteousness is itself a transcendent quality underlying the distinction between evil and good. On a human plane (the level of the "fallen" [broken] created order that is not now what it was created to be) what is, is not always what it ought to be.

It is our human judgment that some chimp behavior looks moral. It's highly doubtful if the chimp has any inkling of its "morality." The chimp is just doing what its genes program it to do. If human morality is predicated on the same natural foundation, human morality is just doing what comes naturally, not doing something that ought to be done. It is this wrongness of the wrong and the rightness of the right that must be explained.

Put in a syllogism, the argument goes like this: There is a difference between right and wrong. Therefore, there is more to reality than matter in motion, that is, there is a transcendent to which matter in motion is morally subject. We call this transcendent God (or a necessary aspect of God). **A simple syllogism**

So, yes, I suppose there is a chimp God "supplying the motivation," that is, a God who has created chimps (perhaps via evolution of a not-totally-naturalistic sort) to be as they are and to display moral-like (if not, strictly speaking, moral) behavior.

What say?

Jim

5

Animal Morality

Dear Carl:

Coincidence? Today I opened my May 10 issue of the *New York Review of Books*. Behold! There was a review of two books: Marc Hauser's *Moral Minds: How Nature Designed Our Universal Sense of Right and Wrong* and Franz de Waal's *Primates and Philosophers: How Morality Evolved*. The reviewer is a professor of European thought at the London School of Economics. The review is worth reading, I think.

Both books take up the issue of human/animal morality, but neither they nor the reviewer does so from a distinctly theistic standpoint. Never is the notion that God might have something to do with morality even mentioned, let alone taken seriously, though there is an acknowledgment of some "medieval" reflection on the subject. The result is that some of the puzzles that can be and have been well addressed by theism remain more puzzling than they need to be.

The existence of the human sense of morality can certainly be addressed; perhaps its connection to animal and human evolution can be at least partially understood. But all one can do is explain the sense of morality, not its actual existence as such. Morality under this condition is not about the actual difference between right and wrong, only the sense that there is a difference. But if all we have is a sense of the difference and not an actual difference, then morality is an illusion: Hitler is as properly moral as Mother Teresa.

Can this be so?

Jim

PART TWO

FROM MORALITY TO WORLDVIEW
The Argument Morphs

Both Carl and Jim had detected that the issue of morality was just the tip of a gigantic iceberg. But it was Carl who first admitted the obvious: their disagreement about animals, humanity and morality was based on a vast difference between their worldviews—their overall take on reality. Carl thought the gap was unbridgeable. Jim refused to admit this. The stack of emails between them began to grow.

6

Morality, the Divine and Everything Else

Dear Jim:

Alas, our worldviews are so different that the gap may be unbridgeable. Why are people like me so refractory to the concept of the "Divine"? Is it because we're stupid or evil? Just think, if the untold thousands of nonbelievers, including Darwin himself, had just taken the few seconds required to understand arguments like those expressed in your syllogism (no. 4, par. 6) we'd all be saved. How come there seems to be an inverse correlation between belief and educational level, especially in the sciences?[1] A helluva lot of people (many of whom have made the greatest contributions to human enlightenment) are perversely denying themselves access to the joys of a faith-based life and perhaps the afterlife as well. If I were you, I would find it puzzling that God chose you for eternal bliss and left me in the outer darkness; I'm not such a bad guy, fairly moral too.

Worlds of difference

My problem is that I can't see any evidence whatsoever for the existence of an entity beyond the physical universe of which we are a manifestation. Moreover, every single human attribute for which you attempt to concoct a spiritual basis can be explained in "naturalistic" terms. No divine intervention is required to explain any part of evolution. Positing a "directed" evolution doesn't even make any sense; it's merely creationism in disguise. Thus, why would God bother to make man via eons of supposedly directed evolution when he could just form him from the dust of the earth and breathe life into

No evidence for God

---

[1]Edward J. Larson and Larry Witham, "Leading Scientists Still Reject God," *Nature* 394 (1998): 313.

him as the Bible asserts? Of course you could say that God was an experimental breeder like humans who created domesticated animals via directed selection, but that would make him kind of a trial-and-error guy just like you and me. That's the problem with God; he invariably morphs into an entity with likes and dislikes, and needs, and egocentricities (note the commandments) that make him resemble a king with a lot of magic up his sleeves.

Morality needs no supernatural

Regarding morality, again, the concept does not in any way require a supernatural explanation. You seem to posit that morality exists without life. Where is the evidence for that? The moral sense exhibited by sentient beings fosters behavior that perpetuates life. It's abundantly clear from observation and experience that certain types of actions (moral behavior—e.g., the work of Doctors Without Borders) perpetuate life while others (immoral behavior—e.g., the Inquisition) do not. Morality tied to life is no illusion; it's quite tangible and verifiable— it's an outgrowth of evolution. Positing "ultimate" morality leads to the absurd conclusion that morality existed before the appearance of anything that could be affected by it.

Yeah, I know, we're back to God territory. But God is eternal and indestructible, so morality has no relevance to him; it only makes sense when applied to vulnerable entities that can be hurt or helped. So God, the invulnerable, made man, the vulnerable, for what reason again? I keep forgetting. Oh yeah, I remember now what I learned in Sunday school. "God made us to know him, to love him and to serve him in this world, and to be happy with him forever in the next." Sounds like a pretty needy guy, having to actually manufacture an entity that will worship him.

Human suffering

With respect to my question about human suffering in a prior email, I don't want you to explain the existence of evil. If my Sunday school lesson is correct, believers like you are going to be happy with God forever in heaven. How is this possible unless you are walled off from the suffering here on Earth (e.g., Darfur)? Do you think it's moral to assume, or at least hope, that you will be so disengaged? Do you think God is happy? I think that the assumption of a happy afterlife with a happy God is one of the most pernicious aspects of religion because it fosters illogical and escapist thinking such as the "left behind" mentality. The only moral afterlife is one in which you and God are in eternal, apparently helpless, misery at the plight of your earthly descendants. Is this better than post-mortem nonexistence?

Hey, how about that no-hitter!

Carl

7

An Objective Foundation for Morality

Dear Carl:

Your first sentence almost says it all: "Alas, our worldviews are so different that the gap may be unbridgeable." I agree. In my book *Why Good Arguments Often Fail,* difference in worldview is the main *rational* reason I give for the failure of any argument (about anything) to persuade.

I would like to expound on my understanding of worldviews, since I already have written about them (in *Naming the Elephant*). But I'll leave that till later, if ever. Suffice it to say here that to change one's worldview significantly usually takes a major reorientation of the whole worldview because changing one single fundamental notion—such as that there is a God to that there is not—alters almost every other element in the worldview.

The rational role of worldview in successful arguments

I am coming to think that such reorientation is often triggered by signals of transcendence, that is, something that happens in one's life—a sudden gasp of awe at a magnificent mountain scene, ocean shore, a New England maple grove in the fall or a tulip field in Holland in the spring; the glimpse of a newborn grandchild; a performance by Yo-Yo Ma or Itzhak Perlman; an ecstatic experience of love; or an imminent threat of the death of a loved one or oneself. These *signals* may not carry much logical weight, but they get one to doubt something in one's worldview and suggest there may be more (or less) to reality than one has thought. Then one can reflect on one's worldview. Who knows what will happen then? Minds do change at fundamental levels.

A nonrational reason for the failure of a good argument

The other main reason for the failure of good arguments is *nonrational*; it is the refusal to accept an argument that might well be persuasive on worldview (presuppositional) commitments but is rejected for the simple reason that the person who should on rational grounds be persuaded refuses to do so because he or she doesn't want it to be true.

Imagine, for instance, that there are a host of reasons why it would be most wise for Jill not to marry Jack. Let's say Jack is lazy, a liar (he's lied to her many times and she knows it), and he doesn't pay his bills (though he spends enough on alcohol to pay them all and then some). Poor Jill will find herself miserable if she marries him. But she is so infatuated with him that she will not agree that marriage is not wise. She *wants* him.

For now at least, let's put aside the *moral* reason for the failure of arguments. If that is one of the reasons we seem at odds—whether it's from my side or yours or both—let us discover that later (if we ever do). Let's stick with rational reasons; we should be able to come to some sense of what separates our judgments about God, human beings and the universe. (Wow! All that!)

Let me also agree with you that people with widely differing worldviews can do highly moral acts. One does not have to believe in God to do deeds that both of us would consider good. Atheists often act with more moral sensitivity than believers in God (even sensitivity that ought to characterize religious believers but doesn't). No, Carl, you're "not such a bad guy."

Can an atheist be moral?

And let's not take up all the issues you raise in your email. Why not focus on one at a time? In due course I'll be happy to take up every one you raise.

The issue that set off our first emails is whether morality can be explained without assuming the existence of something transcendent that exists outside (beyond) the material realm. One short way to put the issue is this: Can good exist without God (or at least some transcendent moral criterion, one that actually exists as transcendent)? I say no. You say yes.

In an earlier email I tried to explain why I concluded that one could not give such an explanation. The argument was not complicated. As you say, it can be understood in a few seconds. There are probably some good reasons for challenging it. I would be interested in hearing them.

Can good exist without God?

I don't think you gave any reasons that actually tell against my main contention, to wit, that there must be a standard by which our sense of what is right and wrong is finally judged. Short of this all we have are different *senses* of what is right and wrong, such different ones that some of them are contradictory. What allows both of us to say that Hitler's pogrom was wrong—even evil—and that the freeing of those yet to be gassed was good? It was not only Hitler who thought the extermination of the Jews was appropriate (that is, a good). Hitler was, he thought, eliminating the unfit and improving the German human breeding stock. We do not. Why? The answer must be a standard that lies outside the opinions of both Hitler and us. It has to be a standard that rejects some *is* for some *ought* that is not an *is*. In other words, morality cannot actually exist if there is no such standard.

The sense and the content of morality

Notice that I have not argued that the *sense of morality* cannot be at least partially accounted for by evolutionary factors that have a purely natural (material) base. You say, "The moral sense exhibited by sentient beings fosters behavior that perpetuates life." I have no telling reason to disagree.

Doctors Without Borders exhibits a morality built on the value of human life; the Inquisition does not, though there is justification for the Inquisition if one accepts the premise that it is better to be tortured into belief and go to heaven than to die without belief and go to hell. I don't believe that, not because I think there is no hell, but because the sort of belief required cannot be produced by torture. It can be, and more likely is, produced by acts of genuine love, love that looks for the betterment of other human life despite the behavior and belief of that other human life.

But is it not the case that the Inquisition thought it was doing good? The Inquisitors had a sense of morality, a sense of what is good, but it was a perverted sense. By the way, Augustine defines evil as the absence or the perversion of the good. Good can exist without evil (God might be one such who so exists), but evil cannot exist without good. In other words, if there is evil, there is also good, not just the sense of good, but Good in itself. As a Christian would add: This is what we call God.

Back to God territory

You write that my argument that "positing 'ultimate' morality leads to the absurd conclusion that morality existed before the appearance of anything that could be affected by it." Then you note, "Yeah, I know, we're back to God territory." Yes, I agree. We are indeed.

But you follow this with a further consideration: "But God is eternal and indestructible, so morality has no relevance to him; it only makes sense when applied to vulnerable entities that can be hurt or helped." Why does this follow? What could be more glorious than that at the heart of reality is a Really Real that is utterly and eternally Good? In light of the mixture of good and evil we find in our world, what would be the best reason for optimism? Would it not give us hope that time having turned into eternity for his creation would be a "time" or "place" of great joy? In other words, a "heaven"?

At this point in your email you comment on God creating vulnerable entities and that that makes God a "needy guy," etc. I would be glad to respond to this, and will later if you would be willing to hear me out. But I'd rather turn the tables a bit. Focusing on the issue of God and morality, I'd like to ask you several questions.

What is awry with my argument for the existence of a transcendent standard of morality? How does a nontranscendent understanding of morality allow Hitler to be wrong and you and I to be right about the Holocaust? Of course, you and I and most of the world believe the Holocaust to be one of the most evil acts in world history. Your and my sense of morality on this point is close to being universal. Still, it is not universal.

A tough question for naturalists

When one adds immediately relevant issues such as pro-life/pro-choice (a life-and-death issue), the situation becomes not only more complex but also more immediately troubled. If abortion is the taking of a human life, then abortion in effect is murder. If pro-choicers are right, pro-lifers are denying women choice at a deeply personal level. You know how the argument goes. Is anyone right here? Both pro-lifers and pro-choicers think they are right enough to force their view by legislation and punishment for violation. How are such issues to be decided justly?

These several questions really boil down to one: How does naturalism (the notion that no transcendent of any kind exists) explain how what appears to some of us (even most of us) to be evil could really be wrong? Or why is it unnecessary for there to be a standard beyond our disagreements that makes it appropriate for us to believe Hitler to be wrong and us right?

So, what say?

I'll see you this evening at the book club. Rich and Kay are, by the way, with us here in Downers. Still, they may have to return to Mayo Monday. They don't yet have a clear picture of Rich's problem.[2]

Jim

8

Scientists and Religious Commitment

Emails now flew back and forth in cyberspace. At the same time, Jim and his wife had gone to help take care of their son Richard's family while Richard was recovering in the local hospital and then being further examined at Mayo Clinic. Some emails, therefore, pick up issues introduced earlier but not yet addressed. Moreover, they are now consciously addressed to the deep issues that divide worldviews, issues that are related to each other often in complex ways. The issue addressed here, however, is among the less complicated.

Dear Carl:

In an earlier email you asked, "How come there seems to be an inverse correlation between belief and educational level, especially in the sciences?"[3]

Your question assumes evidence that is not present in the

---

[2]Jim's son Richard had hung between life and death for ten days; then the infection finally yielded to antibiotics. Still, he found it necessary to go to Mayo Clinic for confirmation of the value of the therapy prescribed by his local doctors. In their emails, Carl and Jim often mention family matters.

[3]See the discussion in email exchange six (pp. 27–29) and email exchange twenty-two (pp. 87–89).

question itself. That evidence may exist, but I would need to see it and how it was arrived at.

Still, I was reminded of your question when I stumbled on this bit of commentary from the editors of *Scientific American* (October 2006, p. 8):

God and the scientists

> Surveys indicate that scientists are only half as likely as the general public to describe themselves as religious, but 40 percent still do. As Albert Einstein wrote, it takes fortitude to be a scientist—to persevere despite the frustrations and the long lonely hours—and religious inspiration can sometimes provide that strength.[4]

The editors seem to be surprised by the high percentage and attribute it to frustration and loneliness rather than to any *rational* reason. I wonder why. Aren't these scientists also intelligent?

Of course, truth cannot be determined by vote. So one should not make too much of a preponderance of nonbelief among scientists or the presence of belief among scientists either, for that matter. At the moment, what such percentages show is that being a scientist does not seem to be a very large factor in either promoting or discouraging belief.

Once a student at Rose-Hulman, a prestigious private engineering college, asked me this after I had given a presentation of the rationality of Christian faith: "Why do you trouble us here at this scientific school? We don't have much use for religion here. You should give your talk at a liberal arts school, where it would find a more ready reception."

What he did not realize is that there are far more university professors of science and the technical fields who are willing to be identified as Christian believers than there are professors of humanities and the social sciences. In other words, Rose-

---

[4] Also see Alister McGrath and Joanna Collicutt McGrath, *The Dawkins Delusion?* (Downers Grove, Ill.: InterVarsity Press, 2007), pp. 41-47.

Hulman, as reluctant as some of the students might be to consider the virtues of Christian faith, was a venue more likely to find the presentation of some value.

In pursuit   My explanation for this greater presence of Christian be-
of truth   lievers in science is that the scientists have not given up on the search for truth. In the present postmodern atmosphere of the humanities and social sciences, skepticism reigns.[5] No one can really *know* the truth about much of anything. As philosopher Richard Rorty puts it, "Truth is what our peers will let us get away with saying." That is, truth is what is said in the language accepted by one's colleagues.[6] Most natural scientists have not bowed the knee to such skepticism. They still consider language representational—that it actually says something about something that really is something and not just a verbal construct. So I'd rather try to dialogue with a natural scientist than a social scientist (the word *science* no longer fits many of them).

See you tonight!

Cheers!

Jim

---

[5] The paucity of vocal Christians in the humanities and social sciences is not new. When these disciplines were modern, as opposed to postmodern, they adopted the scientific assumption that the *true* explanation for all social phenomena is to be found in nature, not in the supernatural. God and the supernatural might or might not exist, but the academic disciplines have no way of detecting them. One could not discover God's existence by the use of reason, but one could explain the belief in the existence God by purely social or psychological, that is, natural, factors. Religion courses became studies in what people believed and the natural reasons why. Theology and the study of religion became sociology or psychology.

[6] See Alvin Plantinga's analysis of Rorty's notion that "truth is what our peers will let us get away with saying" in *Warranted Christian Beliefs* (New York: Oxford University Press, 2000), pp. 429-36.

9

A Colloquy on Morality

The following section is a composite of several emails that moved back and forth between Carl and Jim. It addresses issues raised in emails number four to seven. The form here imitates the give-and-take of semiformal debate.

Carl: With regard to our little colloquy on morality, I don't understand why it's necessary to overlay a perfectly clear and rational Darwinian explanation for the existence of morality with the dross of a supernatural übermorality. It's just superfluous. It doesn't matter that people who do bad things think they are doing good, just as the good people do. From an evolutionary standpoint, the bad people's actions, not their thoughts, are inimical to the survival of the species. Thus, if Hitler's behavior would be generalized to the whole of humanity, the species would die out. It would be no different from the consequences of any species turning upon itself in generalized lethal attack. Such biological mistakes are weeded out in natural selection. Of course, selection is a long-term and imperfect process, so some weediness remains in all species. In short, the "standard by which our sense of right and wrong is finally judged" is whether a given type of behavior promotes or imperils the survival of humanity in all its biological and cultural richness, a purely naturalistic Darwinian standard.

Jim: I think I may surprise you here. I actually agree with you. The notion of a morality deriving from materialist evolution is indeed based precisely where you say it is—on the continued existence of the human part of the biosphere. It assumes that morality functions as a way of keeping human

Übermorality: yes or no

beings in existence. And, I presume, it functions in the same way with any animal species in which some altruistic-seeming care must be taken to preserve its progeny long enough for it to produce its own progeny.

Survival: the final value? But, is it not the case that this assumes that existence of the species—in our case, *homo sapiens*—is better than its nonexistence? In general, that is, existence is better than nonexistence. Human value [in this case] comes simply from its existence. In short, for humans it is better to exist than not exist. But better for what sort of human to exist? The individual or the species? One's own tribe? Or all tribes?

Or, more existentially relevant, what of those who insist on constructing some weapon of ultimate destruction or almost ultimate destruction? Or those who try to prevent this? If the former continue to exist, they may become the only humans who remain. The evolutionary ethic will have worked out in their favor. Those with more altruistic notions of the equal value and dignity of all human beings and the equal worth of every life will have disappeared. The terrorists will then be morally superior to their opponents. Does this make sense? Is this really what we think of as an example of morality, either in action or in theory?

It would then make no sense to say that though there are no (or very, very few) things that are worth killing for, there are some (or maybe many) things that are worth dying for.

In other words, naturalism cannot support an ethic that says there really are some *is*es (like a world where the only thing that makes people valuable is that they are among the *fittest* who have survived) that *ought* not to be. To repeat, some current *is*es (e.g., the terror of the Taliban) *ought* not be. Survival itself has become the ultimate value.

The bottom line is this: if evolution explains what morality is (rather than how the sense of morality came to be), survival itself is either *the* final transcending value (which it can't be for a naturalist) or an utterly inadequate candidate for the foundation of morality. But who would choose survival itself as a candidate for final value? Some might do so, but I suggest that they might only be those persons who finally choose survival for themselves alone. Are there not some things worth dying for?

Carl: I like the first few sentences of your reply [above], down to the sentence beginning with "But, is it not the case . . . " Then you lose me.

Yes, survival is the final value

For any living species, evolution has selected for characteristics that promote its survival. Humans are in no way different from any other species in this regard. The basic tenet of evolution is that it is undirected for all species, including us. A number of mutations along our evolutionary path have enhanced our brains to the extent that we can anticipate our ultimate fate, leading the majority of us to concoct myths to counteract the terror that this knowledge evokes. We can articulate the notion that it's better to exist than not exist, but this sentiment is simply a distillation of the survival mechanism present in all living organisms. Without this mechanism, life would be impossible. So the ascribing of significance to the human preference for existence is pointless.

With respect to the rest of your discussion, I have a very simple answer. Survival mechanisms have to be ingrained in all living organisms, else they would cease to exist; hence in your terms survival *is* the ultimate value. With respect to social animals such as humans, productive social interactions are essential for the survival of the species. Humans who are preoccupied with killing other humans or are constitutionally unable to feel concern for the general welfare tend to be detrimental to this survival and are held in check by those who are not so afflicted. If the baddies you describe engaged in their nefarious activities, either for the pleasure of killing other humans or as a consequence of their pathologically narrow self-interest, and if they became dominant, humanity would die out.

On the other hand, if the majority of these people were motivated by a desire to resist perceived repression (e.g., the Palestinians vis-à-vis the Israelis), their ranks would not be dominated by sociopaths—so even if this category of baddies prevailed, checks and balances would eventually be restored.

The bottom line is this: within a relatively stable physical environment, natural selection leads to the extinction of a species in which self-destructive tendencies prevail, and it favors the survival of a species that creates a cultural environment that fosters the realization of that species' potential. Morality is intrinsic to the evolution of social beings; it's a purely naturalistic phenomenon. There is no demonstrable need of a supernatural source for "oughtness."

Ciphered nihilism

Jim: Your argument is impeccable. Your conclusions follow from your premises. The problem is that what you are describing is nihilism—the inability to distinguish between that which *is* from that which *ought* not to be. Whatever promotes continued existence is the only thing that counts for being good. That is, *is* is all there is. There is no *ought*.

Perhaps all we disagree about is whether morality actually exists. I say it does (there is a difference between what there *is* and what there *ought* not to be). You don't seem to think so.

I just have a hard time believing that you actually believe that. You surely don't act like it. You show, for example, lots of compassion for the continued welfare of those you love. Is that compassion, that love, all just *machinery?* Wouldn't that compassion, that love, be good even if it did not promote the survival of your loved one, the survival of yourself or the survival of the human race?

Tethered to the natural world

Carl: I guess I'm just tethered to "natural world" logic. According to this logic, morality only exists when there are entities that can be affected by it; it's an emergent property of the evolution of social beings. It's a category of behavior, so something has to exist that can exhibit this behavior. Was there morality on the pre-biotic earth? It seems illogical to think so.

You seem aghast at the prospect that compassion and love are just "machinery." I am not aghast; this is apparently where we part company. As long as you cling to the notion of Cartesian duality (for which there is absolutely no evidence), we will be attempting to communicate across an unbridgeable gulf. It's puzzling to me why you require an external (i.e., supraphysical) source for higher cognitive functions. Everything we've learned indicates that this is not the case. Education should wean us away from the belief in spirits.

Jim: Yes, I suppose we are at an impasse, or very close to one. Both of us are "tethered" to different assumptions (convictions, if you will, that strictly can't be proven). Every argument by finite beings such as us is rooted in these convictions. Of course, these conviction can be changed. People are "converted" all the time from Christian faith to something else (naturalism, pantheism, deism, etc.) and from naturalism to Christian faith. Antony Flew has recently been "converted" from atheism (or perhaps strong agnosticism) to deism by philosophers and scientists who believe in intelligent design (thought by scientists like Dawkins to be quite foolish). If you'd like to see the documentation for this, let me know. I don't have it on the tip of my typing fingers, but I can get it.[7]

---

[7] The validity of this conversion is contested. See Antony Flew and Gary Habermas, "My Pilgrimage from Atheism to Theism," *Philosophia Christi* (Winter 2004) <www.biola.edu/antonyflew/flew-interview.pdf>; Gary Habermas, "Antony Flew's Deism Revisited," *Philosophia Christi*, vol. 9, no. 202 (2007) <www.epsociety.org/library/printable/28.pdf>; and Mark Oppenheimer, "The Turning of an Atheist," *New York Times Magazine,* November 4, 2007 <www.nytimes.com/2007/11/04/magazine/04Flew-t.html>.

PART THREE

THE THEOLOGICAL DIMENSION

God in the Dock

Issues of morality soon raise issues of theology. In the following emails, Carl argues that the Christian God whom Jim proposes as a proper foundation for morality is himself neither capable nor worthy of this task. Jim more than demurs.

10

Good and Evil
and the Character of God

Dear Jim:

Okay, the foregoing argument [for a natural explanation of morality] works for me, but evidently not for you. So I'm going to try an ascent into the twilight zone of religious irrationality and approach the argument from your perspective. I'm out of my depth here, so this will not be pretty. Anyhow, let's address the heart of your assertion: "What could be more glorious than that at the heart of reality is a Really Real that is utterly and eternally good?"

The problem I have with this viewpoint is that it doesn't comport with logic or the way things work in the natural world. Monopolarity is a supremely unstable state in the material universe and logically incompatible with any type of existence, mortal or Divine. You posit an invulnerable being that is eternal and perfect. This monopolar being faces none of the negatives that impel us to action; i.e., he has no need for physical or intellectual sustenance, no need to reproduce and no fear of destruction. He would not change.

If you examine the characteristics of this being, you will see that they actually describe nonexistence, i.e., death. The monopolar God you posit would be inert and undetectable because he would have no need to interact with anything or do anything. What could possibly generate a call to action under such circumstances?

If you think I'm blowing smoke here, try a thought experiment. Imagine that the universe is filled with invulnerable, eternal, perfect beings. (I guess this would be one possible view of heaven.) Would it be abuzz with activity and happiness? Why? What would be on the agenda? Becoming more perfect? I think an honest analysis of this state of affairs reveals an unbroken stillness, a blankness, namely the eternal nonbeing that awaits believer and unbeliever alike.

Carl

Emails are now flying back and forth, making it difficult to untangle the argument. The form of this section is, therefore, again recast as informal debate. Jim, responding to the above email, speaks first.

Religious irrationality

Jim: First, I reject your characterization that my perspective involves "religious irrationality." If I grant that, there is no reason for us to continue a dialogue, no hope of either of us changing our mind by being convinced by rational discourse. All we can do is state our positions and let it go at that. I would want us both to understand that matters (such as a foundation for what we both agree is morality) may not be reducible to the canons of human reason, but this does not mean they are in "the twilight zone of religious irrationality." Issues of transcendence, issues of the existence or nature of God, are not necessarily *irrational*. In fact, there are many matters that cannot be so reduced—like our appreciation of a Bach cantata, a Monet haystack or a mother's love for her newborn child. It is not irrational to appreciate art, to love our children or to give our life for that of another; but each of them is more than merely rational.

Carl: But there's no need to invoke any supernatural source for these attributes. Following the logic of evolution explains them nicely.

That said, let me continue the conversation.

Please accept my apologies for the inappropriately flippant tone of my "twilight zone" remark. I was infected by Dawkins.

Jim: One thing on which We do agree: we [agree that we] part company on a very basic primary assumption. I say the

God revealed in the Bible exists and build from that.

Carl: My intrinsic skepticism, reinforced by my professional training, gives me a problem right off the bat. How trustworthy is the Bible? For example, the story of Genesis, the Garden of Eden and the Flood bear considerable resemblance to stories in the Epic of Gilgamesh, an ancient Mesopotamian religious myth. From what little I've read, borrowings from pagan religions permeate the Bible, including the New Testament. Are the events depicted in the Bible based on eyewitness accounts? Where is the scholarly rigor we demand of modern-day historians? Why is the Bible any more valid than the sacred Hindu text—the Bhagavad Gita, for example? Why haven't you embraced Mormonism? After all, Joseph Smith is practically a contemporary; his account of visitations by the angel Moroni seems as credible as any revelations depicted in the Bible. So the Baroque, if not Rococo, theological edifice you construct seems to me to have a pretty flimsy foundation.

Jim: I believe that, though I cannot (nor can anyone) give a knock-down argument (one utterly incontrovertible by any reasonable person) for God's existence. That is, neither I nor anyone else can, strictly speaking, prove the existence of God (or any kind of transcendent being). Still, there are many good reasons for believing that such a God exists; this means that my faith in such a God is characterized by both *faith* and *reason;* it is a *reasonable faith.*

Reasonable faith

Carl: To me, a "reasonable faith" is one that is based on evidence. I have faith that I will see daylight tomorrow morning, assuming that I survive the night. Your claim of reasonable faith in the existence of God has no evidentiary support.

Jim: You start with a commitment either that God does not exist or that his existence is so unlikely that it is safe to assume that he does not exist. At times you seem to suggest that maybe God exists. . . .

Atheism assumed

Carl: This is only because I was trying to argue within your framework. From my standpoint, God does not exist.

Jim: . . . But, you say, because of evil in the world, he is not the sort of God who is worthy of honor.

A search for common ground

Given this, much of our dialogue will have to recognize that it will be hard to find enough common ground for an argument for or against God's existence or the necessity of his existence, if we are to explain the existence of evil (not just our sense of evil). Nonetheless, there are two ways we can converse: (1) we can challenge the internal coherence of each other's views (that's what I have tried to do with regard to morality: to wit, naturalism does not provide an adequate explanation for the actual existence of either good or evil; nor does it give us a foundation for adjudicating between opposing views of what is good [e.g., pro-life or pro-choice]), and (2) we can take some of the matters on which we actually agree (e.g., both of us believe murder is wrong and saving life is right) and see which of the explanations we give for this common idea are better and why we think them better.

The common ground we share with all humanity—that everyone has a sense of morality—seems to me to be a particularly fruitful issue. We haven't succeeded in getting very far. But there is yet some hope one or both of us will change our minds or at least come closer to each other's view. Morality is a profoundly important issue, not just for the two of us but for the continued existence of people in all the societies of the world.

First, let me try to clarify what I posit.

Theism assumed

Yes, God is monopolar, at least in the sense that nothing other than God exists absolutely and eternally: he "has no need for physical or intellectual sustenance, no need to reproduce and no fear of destruction." Agreed. Whether he could change or not is an issue dealt with in Christian theology.

Some theologians influenced by Greek philosophy would say God is "impassible."[1] But no, God (at least the God of the Bible) is not monopolar in the sense that he can have no passions. The problem is that your monopolar description of God does not fit the God who reveals himself in the Bible.

Carl: Quite so. My monopolar description of God follows from "natural world" logic. Thus, if you were the only entity in existence and you were eternal, invulnerable and perfect, it follows from natural-world logic that you would have no needs or desires; ergo, you would be inert. The biblical account departs from this logic train and creates an anthropomorphic God—i.e., a God in the image of man and who therefore has humanoid emotions, even though he has no need of them.

Jim: The God of the Bible is both *personal* and triune.

Carl: Of course. God would be of no psychological value if you didn't have the assurance that he was "there for you." Regarding God's "triuneness," didn't he have to wait for full validation of that aspect of his being until the Council of Nicaea in 325?

Jim: First, as *personal*, God is depicted as reacting to the actions of his creation (especially humans), even changing his mind. On the one hand, he is said both to love his human creation and to show his wrath against evil. He displays his frustration with the people to whom he has revealed himself. Now, you may think that this is not worthy of a God who is perfect (as the Bible also affirms), but the Bible does not think so. The Bible's language about God is, of course, anthropomorphic (i.e., analogical; God's love is *like* but not *identical to* human love or, perhaps put better, we humans are made in his image; our love is in the image of his love). In any case the God of the Bible is not a mere abstraction; he is personal.

God is personal

Carl: The foregoing paints a picture of an entity that shows

Anthropomorphism

---

[1]See, for example, <www.firstthings.com/article.php3?_article=2262 or <www.theism.info/impassibility.html>.

all the attributes of a human being (except, of course, for all the magical power). I can't decipher who is made in the image of whom. (Is that good English?)

Jim: Since God is both transcendent and personal, his goodness (without the necessity of there being any evil) is the standard of reference for human goodness. This means that, when we do that which does not comport with the good character of God, we not only do wrong, we also offend (sin against) God. Morality, therefore, is not just a game of abstract good and evil (doing what is right [defending life] vs. doing what is wrong [willfully taking life]), it is breaking our personal relationship with God. When our children refuse to obey us when we tell them not to hurt each other, they not only do what they should not do, they break their proper relationship with us. We are God's children.

Carl: So we're God's family? He seems to be having the same problems with us that any *pater familias* has with his family. Did he foresee this, or did he just take a chance like the rest of us do? I can't see any divine attributes here except for the size of the family and the magical powers of the papa. Given the travails of his children down through history, God needs to read a good book on parent effectiveness training.

Jim: As Pascal put it, the one true and eternal God is not "the God of the philosophers." This struck Pascal as a result of his "night of fire," his experience of God that he memorialized on a small sheet of paper he sewed into his jacket.

Carl: Is Pascal the one who said that it's better to hedge your bets and believe? In my humble opinion, God would take a pretty dim view of that self-serving rationale. Principled nonbelief should be more forgivable to God than calculated belief, although I shouldn't presume to project my own moral precepts on a God I don't believe in.

God is triune   *Jim:* Second, God is triune. The Christian doctrine of the Trinity—the church's understanding of the Bible's depiction of God—means that he is a complex of three persons in one. As Trinity, God is not monopolar. I know that this is not a concept that readily yields to our human understanding. I do not expect you to believe that such a God exists, but I would like you to see why it is that, given such a God, Christian belief about God providing the foundation for morality is actually rational. In any case, the doctrine of the Trinity is the traditional way of understanding how God has revealed himself. Theologians say it explains why for God there is no need to create. He already exists with plurality; he is not a singular digit, such as the god (Brahma) of the Hindu Advaita Vedanta tradition.

Carl: You're snowing me here. I got lost in the rationale for the Trinity as the basis for the foundation of morality. But I like the part about the Trinity showing that God has no need to create. I was already convinced of that from my monopolarity argument.

Jim: In any case, there is no reason why God cannot choose to create if he wishes.

God is free to create

Carl: But why would he wish to unless he's dissatisfied with the status quo? How is that possible in a perfect entity? Having God wishing for something is just loading him down with another human attribute.

Jim: God is only limited by what would be self-defeating or stupid, like being unable to make a stone he could not lift (intrinsic self-contradiction); i.e., God can't go against his own character of goodness (the foundation for our human ethics) and of rationality (the foundation for our human rationality).

Carl: Creating humanity seems pretty self-defeating and stupid. What did he expect would happen, given the parameters he laid out? Was he looking for trouble (or perhaps a good show)? Why didn't he just make more angels?

God, self-defeating and stupid—or richly relational?

Jim: There is no *blankness* to God's character, as you say, and certainly no *deadness*. There is rather a richness of relationship. That relationship is deep enough to preserve. When it is preserved or when our offense against God is forgiven, a heaven-like happiness is the result. Thus the Bible talks about heaven in terms of joy and rejoicing. Heaven is not eternal stillness and is never depicted as such in Scripture. God is never depicted as abstractly monopolar; he is both one and many (three-in-one); there is personal interaction between the persons of the Trinity.

Granted, the Trinity is a notion that is beyond reason without being *unreasonable* (i.e., irrational). The Trinity is, I think, not a notion that a philosopher would ever imagine or wish to argue for. I wouldn't anyway. But Christians take that notion as the best way of understanding the way God is presented in the New Testament, which they also take as worthy of belief (they have justification for that belief too).

More anthropo-morphism *Carl:* The foregoing is another anthropomorphic depiction of God (leaving out the Trinity business, which in my admittedly humble opinion just fogs things up). In any case, this depiction reveals to my jaundiced eye a rather malign attribute of God. God endowed humans with the power to offend him so that he can have the option to forgive them or not. I see no beneficent motive in this; it seems rather to be a cruel game invented to relieve the boredom of drowning in perpetual goodness. As I've asked in my email, would God have preferred that humans, despite their capacity, never offended him so he would never have to forgive or not forgive? If he's all good, he should be happy for such lack of offense, but then what would be his net accomplishment, more joy and happiness? He already has a surfeit of those. The creation of man only makes sense if he offends God and God expected him to do so.

Science or reasonable faith *Jim:* Of course, the Christian understanding of God rests on revelation found in the Bible. Its authority is accepted on faith, sometimes by some on *blind faith*. But faith is not necessarily blind. There is such a thing as *reasonable faith*, that is, faith for which one can find some (maybe many) reasons to think it is well placed. But then science, too, is based on faith, not *blind faith* but *reasonable faith*.

There are good reasons for thinking that the universe is uniform (but there is no final proof). There is reason to think that the five senses give us good information about what is out there beyond ourselves (but no final proof that we are not dreaming). So both science and modern naturalism (the idea that there is no spiritual reality) require commitment beyond what is, strictly speaking, provable. Let's not denigrate each other for disagreeing on which assumptions are most likely to be true. We both make such judgments. We both are equally likely to make mistakes.

Carl: No way, man! Science is based on evidence, not faith. The good reason for thinking that the universe is uniform is based on a tremendous number of observations. Ditto for the "faith" in the five senses. There is no evidentiary counterpart in religion. Attempting to equate the way science and religion arrive at their respective worldviews is pure sophistry.

11

God Almighty

Carl continues his critique of the character of God, this time raising questions about God's goodness, his power, his demand to be worshipped and his need to create.

Carl: Another problem with your argument [for God as the foundation of morality] is that if God is perfectly good, he cannot be omnipotent, since evil exists in your worldview.

So if God is to maintain his unsullied image, there has to be a Not God and a Not Heaven that coexists with him. On the other hand, if God is omnipotent and doesn't have to contend with a Non-God (evil) entity, then he must embody evil as well as good within himself. Dipolarity has to get in there somehow. So if evil exists, I don't see how God can be perfectly good and omnipotent simultaneously. I think you want God to be omnipotent, so you have to allow some evil into his character. This would seem to be at odds with the monopolar goodness of your "Really Real." A God with bad as well as good attributes does seem reasonable, however, given his egocentricity and vindictiveness as chronicled in the Bible (along with his decent attributes, of course).

Jim: There are several strands of argument here, and I need to untwist them so that each can be treated on its own; then I will comment on the cord itself.

The age-old problem of evil— the gory Christian solution

Strand one is the standard problem of evil, expressed largely as it has been for what—centuries? My answer to this problem includes several key elements. The first involves the *free will* response. In short, if human beings were to be given the freedom to make choices for which they are ethically responsible, and thus truly be able as finite creatures to do good, they must also be able to choose to do evil.

Carl: As I asked above, why would God indulge in this nasty little game? Presumably, things were fine in heaven before he set all this up (or were they?). Man had to be able to choose to do evil so God could have the satisfaction of rewarding those who choose to do good. Why go through all this? Will the joy experienced by those who choose to do good surpass the joy of those already in heaven, never having had to make a choice (angels, for example)? Moreover, the suffering of innocent humans (not involved in these choices—small children, for example) down through the ages as a consequence of this God-engendered scenario makes him look pretty bad in my book.

Jim: The second key element is God's willingness to suffer himself the pain of atoning for the sins of humankind. He has taken on himself the consequences of what we did with the freedom given us.

Carl: Again, would God have preferred that man never sinned? What's the point of the whole exercise if that were the outcome? God's alleged suffering in this context makes him sound like a sadomasochist.

Jim: In the final analysis from a Christian point of view, the significance of the crucifixion solves the problem as well as we human beings can have it solved this side of glory when we will be able to understand much more than we do now about who God is and why the world has gone through such tragic-seeming events. I have written on this in chapter thirteen of my book *Why Should Anyone Believe Anything at All?* I would be happy to put in your hands (gratis) a copy of this book, if you'd be willing to read at least that chapter.

Carl: The blood sacrifice of the crucifixion is uncomfortably reminiscent of similar rituals in pagan religions, despite the gloss you put on it. I can't see how the brutality of this whole exercise can be given a positive spin. Of course there's the resurrection, so we needed the crucifixion, which in turn required the betrayal by Judas (who really got a bad rap here, I think). I'm sorry, but from the viewpoint of an atheist, this whole business is pretty uncivilized.

Jim: The free-will response does not require a person to be a Christian in order to *see* the relevance of such an answer. The significance of the crucifixion is another matter. To see why it is so central to a response to the problem probably will require a person to already be a Christian believer or to walk a few miles in the moccasins of a Christian believer. What I mean by this is that the event and meanings of the crucifixion carry a profound load of weight for those who have a profound grasp of God's goodness and his righteousness, as well as a profound understanding of the sinfulness of sin. So, just for the sake of understanding me, try to walk in a Christian's shoes.

Carl: Sorry, the goodness and righteousness doesn't mix very well with all the blood and gore. What I'm getting is a profound understanding of the sinfulness of God, the architect of this whole sordid mess. I apologize if you are offended, but this is a sincere response. Just think about how this alleged happening led to the persecution of the Jews as "Christ-killers."

Jim: By the way, I really try to walk in the shoes of those with whom I disagree. One way I do this is to keep reading the great literature of those who, like Virginia Woolf, Bertrand Russell and Richard Dawkins, are naturalists.

Carl: Evidently you are immune to the blandishments of these apostates. I've read a lot of Bertrand Russell and find him quite convincing.

Dipolar or monopolar God?

Jim: *Strand two* takes us back to our disagreement over a monopolar/dipolar God. Here I think we may be able to make some progress. For one thing, I have already commented about a monopolar God. Those remarks stand. To wit, God does not have to be monopolar to be a unity of one and many (i.e., the Trinity).

Moreover, Christians have rarely (at least since Augustine) thought that to be infinitely good, there must be something or someone to contrast to his goodness. Augustine maintained (and the church has mostly followed him in this) that evil is not something in itself: it is not something or someone. Evil is *moral*, not *metaphysical*. Evil exists when someone violates the good, that is, when a human person or an angel (also a good creation of God) chooses to disobey God. Evil is therefore good perverted. Goodness can exist without evil; evil cannot exist without good.

Carl: Imagine that. An angel, one of God's task force, choosing to do evil, presumably while in heaven and in the very presence of God! How could that be possible? What more could an angel want than to be continually joyful and happy in the presence of God? Is there dissatisfaction in heaven? Does that mean that after you die and go to heaven you can still choose to do evil? What are the consequences? If all this can happen, how does heaven differ from this mortal coil? Finally, if all this can happen in heaven can you really be sure that God is not just a little tainted? At the very least he has his hands full dealing with evil in paradise as well as on earth.

Jim: Strand three is your declaration that God as displayed in the Bible has characteristics of both good and evil. This charge has, of course, been frequently made before. It is in some ways a hard one to deny, for we do find God doing what seems to us to be unjustified violence to innocent people.

Is God both good and evil?

Well, I have also responded in print to this notion. And rather than repeat what I have written, I will attach it to this email.[2] It is a section from my book *Learning to Pray Through the Psalms* and comes in a commentary on Psalm 137 that glories in God's dashing on rocks the babies of Israel's enemies. The psalm, which begins in a plaintive lament that tears at the reader's heart, ends with this grisly vision. One way around seeing God as unusually vindictive is to charge the ancient

---

[2]This attachment was an excerpt from *Learning to Pray Through the Psalms* (Downers Grove, Ill.: InterVarsity Press, 2005), pp. 154-67. It can be summarized as follows: five factors intertwine to explain why the psalmist may appropriately pray these awe-full words: (1) the utterly infinite holiness (separateness and righteousness) of God far exceeding our ability to comprehend; (2) in the light of God's holiness, the utter wretchedness of our moral character, that is, the sinfulness of our sin; (3) the utter justice of God's judgment; (4) the historical reality of the violent, unjust destruction of Jerusalem by the foreign armies of Babylon linked with the Hebrew people's sense of destiny as God's people; (5) the fact that the prayer calls for God's vengeance rather than their own; (6) the accurate depiction of the state of the psalmist's desire and the desire of any human being at any time reflecting on the wicked deeds that have been done to them; (7) the situation of the psalm in the biblical revelation, which when it is brought into the context of the atoning sacrifice of Jesus finds its bitter vindictiveness replaced by forgiveness.

psalmist with being too sinfully human. That's what C. S. Lewis does. But I don't take that tack.

Again, let me plead patience here for the ancient Israelites and for modern Christians who wish to pray the prayers of the ancients. From the inside of faith, what appears to be a dishonorable action of God may rather be (1) honorable from the point of view of an utterly righteous God who is responding to utterly despicable evil or (2) something we simply do not yet have the ability to understand. God is, after all, infinite in his goodness (and hatred of sin) as well as infinite in his mercy (and love for the sinner). Again, the cross addresses this.

Carl: It's a grisly vision, all right. God's nastiness seems to be giving you some problems here. It's a good thing that the cross addresses this, because logic doesn't seem to.

A groveling prayer By the way, how about that Lord's Prayer? If you parse it, it's just one big grovel. Do you really have respect for a God that expects such obedience from you? But I digress.

Jim: Yes, it is a digression and is really off point. What is it the logicians say about the fallacy of many questions? Who do Christians say God is? Who do they believe humans are? The Lord's Prayer is one of the best and tiniest capsules of what the Christian faith consists in.

When, as an elder of First Presbyterian Church, I have spoken with would-be members of our congregation, I've used it, along with the Apostles' Creed, as a summary of the basic teachings of our church. We expect every member to affirm it, not because as a local body of believers we enforce it, but because it was, in Jesus' time (and still is two thousand years later), central to what he taught. It's the prayer he gave his closest followers. Groveling? Come on!

Carl: Okay, I'm coming on. What is the teaching in this prayer? There's only one mildly moral admonition in it—the phrase "as we forgive our debtors." The rest is obeisance, pure and simple—praising and asking. Does God need this?

12

God, His Human Creation and Heavenly Bliss

Carl continues to launch a frontal attack on the character of God, now questioning his motives, his intelligence and his sense of justice.

Carl: So, what are the implications of the foregoing arguments for the relationship between God and humankind? First, God had to desire to create humans, indicating he was not satisfied with the status quo (a sign of imperfection?). Second, he had to make humans lesser beings. (Why would he just make more of himself?) Third, he had to give humans intelligence, curiosity and the capacity for independent judgment; otherwise he would just be creating a batch of two-legged slugs (not too exciting for him). Fourth, he needed to have these created beings participate in a scenario of which he could not know the outcome. (What would be the point of creating these beings if they just gathered around him singing hymns of praise or if he knew the outcome of their actions? Boring!) I bet God was biting his celestial fingernails through the whole apple episode in the Garden of Eden. What if Adam and Eve had resisted temptation and simply continued gamboling innocently about at the feet of God? Major divine disappointment here! But luckily they didn't, and we were off to the races.

Jim: Well, what a bunch of charges!

First, no, God did not have to create. He was complete in himself (see my previous comments about the Trinity). Some have suggested that he created in order to share his glory and his joy among others than himself. That is, he created out of generosity.

(All that is speculation, however—just a possibility. Except

God as creator

in answer to your charge, I make nothing of it.)

Carl: God created the nightmarish scenario that we've already discussed (the choice between good and evil, rewards and punishments, etc.) in order to share his glory and joy? I'm glad you make nothing of it.

Jim: Second, of course God's creation would be lesser. But isn't it amazing that he made a finite universe so amazing? Many scientists are as amazed at what they see in the universe as they are in what they understand. Example: Loren Eisley.

Carl: I'm duly amazed at the wonder of the universe without the necessity of invoking a maker.

Jim: Third, I wouldn't quite put it the way you do, but you are essentially correct here [that God created intelligent, curious human beings who could exercise judgment and make responsible choices].

God's foreknowledge of tragedy and pain

Fourth, God's foreknowledge about what will happen may or may not be complete. Theologians disagree. I think God did in fact know that his creation would cost him pain. Somewhere the New Testament says that Christ was slain "before the foundations of the world."[3] That may mean he knew the world was in for a long history of pain and suffering—as was he. I am on the edge of my ability to imagine let alone be sure of just what to believe.

What I do believe however is that God knew what he was doing, and it was better to create us than not to create us. Maybe here is a small point of agreement with your take on morality, that it is better to be than not to be, that is, that existence itself is a value, though I would want to distinguish between what might continue to exist (various totalitarian worlds in which everyone is tortured but a handful of torturers) and what would be better to exist (a worldwide community of love and respect). But this my old argument revived.

---

[3] See Revelation 13:8.

Carl: I'm too tired (11:00 p.m.) to deal with all the vagaries of the foregoing paragraph. I will say, however, that if God knew what was going to happen as a result of his machinations, there would seem to be no reason to undertake the project. If he didn't know precisely what would happen but set things up in a manner that ensured that something definitely would happen (choice between good and evil), then I am confirmed in my atheism because the only logical reason for providing the opportunity for evil is the anticipation that some evil will occur; otherwise everything remains as before. This is not a God with whom I would wish to be acquainted.

Jim: By the way, C. S. Lewis wrote *Perelandra,* a science-fiction novel in which he depicted a scene on Venus in which his humanlike creation rejected temptation to disobey God. Moreover, the Eastern Orthodox believe that human beings, through living an obedient life, can eventually become what they call *divinized,* that is, like Jesus, the perfect human being.

Carl: My last concern in this exchange is what happens when true believers die. One possibility is that they enter the blankness of a perfect heaven, which is actually the blankness of death faced by us benighted nonbelievers. The other possibility is that they enter the good-bad heaven of a good-bad God, which is kind of like earth with a powerful king, except that it lasts forever. In the latter scenario the true-believing afterlifers would probably be sentient and could be aware of the continued suffering of the mortals, including their direct descendants, back here on God's failed experiment.

When believers die

You agreed with me in our discussion at the wine tasting that God is not happy, presumably because of the ongoing travails of his earthly creatures. What about the rest of heaven's occupants? To experience the total happiness that you're aiming for, they would have to be "cleansed" of prior knowledge of this suffering and protected from any further exposure to it. Don't you think this would be rather tacky, maybe even immoral? The only morally valid state for heaven dwellers would be one of eternal misery in sympathy with those left on earth. You really want to go there?

Jim: Neither possibility you list of what life after death will be like makes any sense in terms of the kind of God Christians believe in. There is not a good-bad God (see my previous comments on your notion of a monopolar/dipolar God); there is likewise no good-bad heaven. So there is nothing here to refute.

I don't remember what I said at the wine tasting about God's not being happy with the travail of his creation. But the Bible does depict Jesus as weeping over Jerusalem because it had disobeyed and rejected God. And it shows Jesus in agony on the cross. Jesus sided with the psalmist, all of Israel and all of his children when he cried out, "My God, my God, why have you forsaken me?" This, theologians say, shows that he was bearing the impossibly painful consequences of human disobedience and thus making possible the reconciliation of God and his creation.

Carl: God needed the crucifixion? Again, how pagan. And now we're all nicely reconciled? I'll take your word for it. But what about my question concerning what the other occupants of heaven are feeling? Can they be happy, given the plight of those still in mortal form?

Jim: Again, let me assure you, I can easily imagine that you will not find this sort of theology attractive. But I believe that it is far more honest about the genuine evil of evil and the goodness of good. And it certainly gives more meaning to the human experience of suffering than the notion that we are momentary beings, as one atheist put it, who exist between two oblivions—nonexistence before birth and nonexistence after death. Rather, we are "created eternities" worthy (by virtue of being created in the image of God) of the death and resurrection of God Incarnate.

Carl: From what I've understood of your exposition, you're welcome to him.

13

God and Human Free Will

Dear Jim:

It seems to me that the essential paradox in the relationship between God and his creations (human beings and angels, assuming he also created the latter) is that he left open the possibility that they could turn away from him, thereby doing evil. In doing this he had to anticipate that some of his creatures would stay with him and some would not. Why would God do this if he is purely good? In effect he is bringing evil into existence by creating the capacity to reject him. Why would he not just stay in perfect solitude, thereby maintaining perfect goodness, or create beings that are also purely good?

A paradox of free will

It seems to me that the only explanation for God's behavior is that he needs to have the company of autonomous entities that choose him when they have the opportunity to reject him, i.e., he needs to be freely loved by entities outside himself. To remain alone or to be surrounded by mindlessly loving creatures must be intolerable even to God. He must take the chance that even angels, who are bathed in the glory of his presence, can and do turn away from him (as could people like you who wind up in heaven).

What is most reprehensible is his anger when he is rejected, given the fact that he made it possible and knew it would happen. Moreover, how is heaven any better than earth if evil can exist equally in both realms? At the end of this logic train we are left with a vulnerable, needy, conflicted, all-too-human

God's anger

God who is to be pitied—and condemned for unleashing so much suffering, but certainly not worshiped.

Carl

14

Speculation   What If? It Seems to Me . . .

Dear Carl:

The problem with speculation The first problem I have in responding is that the challenge you pose is mostly speculative. I do not have a problem with your first premise: the Bible more than suggests that God created what he wanted to create and that he had both the intention and the ability to fully realize his intention. But in Scripture we only have hints as to why he intended what he intended.

The Bible is clear that his original creation (whether material or spiritual) was completely good (see Genesis 1 for material creation). It is also clear from Scripture that whatever God does (or historically did) is and was good. And it is clear from Scripture (and reason) that clear knowledge of why God does what he does must come from God himself. Without revelation from God, the human mind may speculate (i.e., use the human faculties of reason and imagination); in fact, it does this all the time.

I think we agree that the traditional myths of various cultures are evidence of highly creative speculation, at least some of which is misguided if it is intended to be a clue to reality. For Christians, however, unless the Bible seems to be clear on any issue having to do with the nature and character of God, we had best not make too much of our speculation, whether made by Christians or by those who are not.

So when you say, "It seems to me that the only explanation for God's behavior is that he needs to have the company of autonomous entities that choose him when they have the opportunity to reject him, i.e., he needs to be freely loved by entities outside himself," it is not hard for me (or any reasonable person) to ask, "Why is that the only explanation?" Why is it necessary for God to "need" to do something? Human beings do lots of things they do not "need" to do—paint pictures, or even "take" pictures, for example (the list is endless). If we do things we don't need to do, why must God have to have a need?

The Bible does contain at least a hint that God knew what he was doing when he made human beings capable of rejecting him and that he was willing to suffer himself for this decision (according to Revelation 13:8, the Lamb of God [Jesus] was slain "from the foundation of the world"). Now, I know that you think that a God who would create a world in which this sort of solution to the problem of human freedom and rebellion was appropriate is not worthy of worship. But if this part of the human story is placed in the whole scope of a biblical worldview, the objection either becomes weak or disappears entirely.

God's foreknowledge

Look at it this way: in making human beings morally free (they can do the good or not do the good), God gave them a full sense of self, a freedom to be what they should be or not. It was their decision. They made and make the wrong decisions. They should be held responsible for them, or their freedom is a sham. Turning from the good, they not only do the bad, they also become morally corrupt and incapable not only of truly understanding good and evil but also of doing at least some of the good they know they should do. In this process they are alienated from God—the very root of their created-in-the-image-of-God nature.

The value of human freedom

The consequences of human rebellion

The essence of humankind's punishment for sin is their continued separation from God. Hell may be "a place," but if so the essence of that place is "separation from God." God rescues them from this consequence by providing a solution human beings can't provide for themselves. In God's trinitarian aspect, God the Son took on himself the punishment for humankind's rebellion. As Paul says within Romans 5:6-11, "God proves his love for us in that while we were yet sinners, Christ died for us" (verse 8). Here is clearly a sufficient reason to worship God. He not only gave us a marvelous existence, he also kept us from the loss of everything that makes life worth living—a beautiful growing relationship with him and his eternal family. Heaven is no mixture of good and evil; it is no static image on a Greek vase; it's a place of lively goodness and artistic, joyous, eternal creativity.

Now you might say that this biblical perspective is no less speculative than that found in the world's various and contradictory mythologies or in the secularist's purely naturalistic way of explaining our human plight. Here a Christian may reply, "Not really." There is good reason to believe the biblical accounts of God's interaction with human beings from their creation to the first century. Those reasons will have to be addressed later. But they are there.

Justification for belief in the Bible

For me, the focus of the justification of belief in the Bible is the nature and character of Jesus as presented in the Gospels (again, there are good reasons for thinking that the Gospels are not typical myths but narratives of the life, death and resurrection of the incarnate Son of God). But this must wait for another time. I've actually written about this in *Why Should Anyone Believe Anything at All?* I'd be glad to give you a copy, but only if you'll agree to read it.

Jim

15

Carl's Sabbath   **A Personal Reflection**

Dear Jim:

The following are random thoughts that I mulled over as I drove the six hundred miles to PA yesterday.

I'm writing this (surrounded by religious tomes) in the study of Nancy's father, a quite conservative rural Methodist minister (now deceased) for whom I had a great affection because he was a very kind and sweet man. From what I know of his history, he had these attributes throughout his life, both before and after he became a minister. He had three children, Nancy (whom you know), Suzanne and James, all of whom grew up totally immersed in a Christian religious environment that would undoubtedly pass muster before God as you envision him. They were wonderful children who would make any parent proud and, as young believers, willingly gave of themselves to church activities.

My family

In adulthood, Nancy became an outstanding teacher and first-rate scholar with two master's degrees from the U. of Wisconsin, Suzanne obtained a BS in nursing from Columbia University, and James obtained a PhD in philosophy from Temple University. He is on the faculty of the Religion Department at Indiana University of Pennsylvania. All three remain superb human beings; all three are now atheists. All three have told me that the renunciation of religious faith was a mentally emancipating experience (as was the case for me). None of them has lost their innate goodness as a result of this transition.

When I was a grad student in biochemistry at the U. of Wisconsin, I took a course from a world-renowned biochemist and cancer researcher named Van R. Potter. (He was also

Bioethics in graduate school

cofounder of the McArdle Laboratory for Cancer Research at
the University of Wisconsin, one of the most prestigious cancer research institutes in the world.) I was very impressed with
his course and with the qualities I perceived in him as a human
being. His childlike wonderment at the workings of the natural world and his enthusiasm in the quest to understand it were
inspiring. You could meet him in the hall and tell him about
some of your experimental results that you considered interesting. He would invariably share, if not exceed, your excite-
ment and launch into a discussion of the broader implications
of your findings. It was a joy to be in his company.

You may be familiar with the term *bioethics*. He coined this
term in a small book entitled *Bioethics, Bridge to the Future,*
published in 1971. Now there are faculty positions in bioethics
at most major universities. As I indicated earlier, I was drawn
to him because of his personal and scientific qualities. But
that's not all—I heard him deliver a number of talks on science
and religion at various venues in Madison. In his typically
lucid fashion he laid out his arguments for the incompatibil-
ity of these two modes of thinking, to the detriment of the
religious point of view. In sum, he was a profoundly ethical,
moral, kind, generous, exciting, inquisitive and brilliant atheist. Needless to say, I became one of his post-docs.

Among the nonscientists I admire is the great American
poet Wallace Stevens. Being an English professor, you probably know a lot more about him than I do, but I like those of
his poems that I can understand (e.g., "Blanche McCarthy"
and "Of Mere Being"). According to his biography, he was an
atheist till the last moments of his life, at which point he may
have undergone a deathbed conversion, although this is in
some dispute. In any case, if Stevens did turn to God at the last
moment, such a conversion would do no credit to Christianity
or to God. A God that punishes honest nonbelief, thereby elic-
iting such fear-ridden, desperate last-minute appeals would, in

my view, be an egotistical bully that demands unquestioning obeisance. Pascal evidently subscribes to this view of God by advocating the hedge-your-bets strategy for belief.

Okay, where am I going with all this? I guess I'm asking what determines whether a person is going to be good or not? Is religion (particularly Christianity) or the absence thereof the primary determinant? Francis Collins found God as a result of encounters with sick people *in extremis* and the reading of C. S. Lewis. He was undoubtedly happier as a result, but was his "goodness quotient" elevated? One could argue on the basis of his personal history that he was just as good a person before he found God as after, although psychologically less secure.

What determines moral character?

I have given examples of individuals who transitioned from belief to atheism, with similar psychological benefits or who remained lifelong atheists with no psychological or moral decrement. C. S. Lewis is given much credit by Collins for his awakening. I credit the grand old atheist-pacifist Bertrand Russell in large measure for mine. Comparing Lewis and Russell, I think you would have to award the latter a higher position on the gravitas scale (Nobel Prize, coauthor of *Principia Mathematica* and author of *A History of Western Philosophy,* among other substantial works). You said you've read his work. Did you read his autobiography? I read it about thirty years ago, and I recall being struck by the poignancy of his preface. I don't remember his exact words, but he indicated that his life had been ruled by three passions: the quest for knowledge, the search for love and unbearable anguish at the suffering of mankind.

So now we have examples of good Christians who became good atheists and good atheists who became good Christians. (You can provide more examples of the latter.) The constant here appears to be goodness, while the variable is the presence or absence of belief in God. It is reasonable to conclude, therefore, that a person's character is not determined by his religiosity, or lack thereof, but rather by his innate biological makeup.

In this context I join my atheist relatives and friends in being appalled at the capriciousness and barbaric cruelty of God as portrayed in much of the Bible.[4] I think you must concede that you have to do a lot of biblical cherry picking to tease out the God that you think truly embodies your concept of Christianity. Can it be that innately good people (atheists and believers alike) actually have higher standards of morality than those represented in the Bible as a whole? (How did Christ feel about eternal damnation?)

With regard to your possible contention that good atheists have this attribute because they were indoctrinated with Christian ethics, I would argue that ethical codes of conduct are not the sole province of Christianity. Proscriptions against killing, stealing and committing perjury (the only three of the Ten Commandments that can be found in the laws of any modern nation) comprise fundamental rules for the survival of any society and, as I've said before, such ethical precepts must be innate, else great pre-Christian civilizations (e.g., Egyptian and Greek) could never have arisen.

Other man-made myths You know how all the other religions are man-made myths that arose at different times in our history? How come the one true religion resembles all the other mythical ones in this respect? It seemed to appear in some scraggly desert tribe at some given point in time. Did the one true God finally decide that it was time he made an appearance? Why did he allow so much time to elapse, during which myriad other false gods and religions were concocted?

A logically defensible as well as a morally upright God would have been in man's consciousness from the beginning. The gods of the Egyptians, Greeks, Romans, Sumerians, etc.,

---

[4]See Elizabeth Anderson in "Relevant Readings."

were obviously made up in good faith to satisfy man's need to fill gaps in our understanding of the natural world. Why did God allow man to be clueless for so long when he didn't have to? The whole thing looks pretty suspicious to me. The fact that the one true God emerged in the same manner as all the other false gods suggests that he may actually be in the same category as the other deities, i.e., a gap-filling myth.

Now for something completely different (as they used to say on *Monty Python's Flying Circus*).

I may have talked about this in some of our prior exchanges, but here it comes anyway. The "old-earth Christians" who subscribe to the theory of evolution suffer grievously from intellectual and theological inconsistency. One must ask them why an omnipotent God, who presumably had an objective in mind, would sit back and allow random mutations and environmental selection to determine over a time span of billions of years what the outcome would be. This is a disengaged God. Man might never have appeared. Innumerable species emerged and became extinct while God twiddled his thumbs. What's the point? If you argue that God tinkered with evolution so as to engineer the outcome, much like a dog breeder, one must ask why this was necessary. Did he need billions of years of experimentation? That surely argues against his omnipotence.

The "young-earth Christians" exhibit greater consistency in this context. Thus, if you believe in the omnipotence of God, he would have no need of all the folderol of evolution. He would just make man instantly without any time-consuming preamble, just as stated in the Bible. The overwhelming problem with this position, however, is that you're stuck with all the evidence for an old earth and an old universe and have to concoct a trickster God who planted false evidence for evolution to test the faith of his believers (which evidently he must desire to be unquestioning). Since he gave man a brain

Something completely different: evolution and the character of God

designed to base his actions on the evidence gleaned from his surroundings, such deception would seem to be inconsistent at best and highly reprehensible from a moral perspective. So neither old-earth nor new-earth Christianity seems tenable on the basis of natural-world logic.

One must conclude, therefore, that the God concept is not compatible with the way things work in the natural world, no matter what kind of mental contortions one exercises to try to force a fit.

Carl

PART FOUR

INTELLIGENT OR UNINTELLIGENT DESIGN

Jim's casual comment about his dialogue with a proponent of a young earth sparked curiosity from Carl. Jim's lack of conviction about intelligent design may seem out of place in one who defends God as Creator. But let the dialogue continue.

16

Scientists and Intelligent Design

Dear Jim:

You indicated in an earlier email that you are not an adherent of young-earth creationism and yet you bring up intelligent design, which is creationism in disguise. These concepts have been thoroughly discredited, beginning (at least) with Hume and Darwin and continuing to the present day. Did you read the Dover, PA, school board trial transcript in which Behe's testimony regarding "irreducible complexity" was crushed by a mountain of countervailing evidence? Did you read the judge's opinion in which he used the phrase "breathtaking inanity" to describe the intelligent design proponents' case?

The highly regarded Department of Biological Sciences at Lehigh University, in which Behe holds a position, has taken pains, in a written statement, to dissociate itself from him with respect to his positions on intelligent design and irreducible complexity. They do have standards. William Dembski, the "philosopher" of intelligent design, has fared no better; his mathematical arguments have been discredited, and he has moved (with encouragement, I understand) from Baylor University to Southern Baptist Theological Seminary. Please don't say you're tethered to the intelligent design mentality. Please. Please. Please.

My tether connects me to the natural world and the logic that flows from its workings. In this world there is no evidence for ghosts and no need to invoke them—in fact, invoking them is a barrier to understanding. Take the tooth fairy, for example. I assume you've put that belief behind you because it wasn't supported by evidence, and you would agree that continued faith in this entity after reaching maturity is not healthy. I trust you've reached the same conclusion about

Santa Claus, for the same reasons. Now follow this logic up the line through trolls, goblins, witches and their ilk to the hundreds of demigods and gods (such as Aphrodite, Poseidon, Apollo, Zeus and Wotan). All disposed of for lack of evidence. Only one more to go. C'mon, you can do it!

Carl

17

Intelligent Design

Here Jim responds section by section to the previous email, parts of which are reproduced below. That email could have been printed only in form below, but the passionate tone of Carl's comments would have been muted.

Carl: You indicated in an earlier email that you are not an adherent of young-earth creationism, and yet you bring up intelligent design, which is creationism in disguise.

Jim: That ID is creationism in disguise is a common charge made by naturalistic evolutionists, but it is simply not true. Carl, it is absolutely necessary that you take the description of ID as the ID people themselves present it. Stick with the descriptions given by philosophers, scientists and scholars associated with the Discovery Institute. Especially relevant is chapter three, "Scientific Creationism: Is Intelligent Design a cleverly designed form of scientific creationism?" in *The Design Revolution.*[1]

---

[1] William Dembski, *The Design Revolution* (Downers Grove, Ill.: InterVarsity Press, 2004), pp. 41-44; see also David DeWolf et al., *Traipsing into Evolution: Intelligent Design and the Kitzmiller vs. Dover Decision* (Seattle: Discovery Institute Press, 2006).

The answer is an unambiguous no.

Carl: These concepts have been thoroughly discredited, beginning (at least) with Hume and Darwin and continuing to the present day.

Jim: Certainly, ID was not discredited by Hume. It did not exist until the late 1980s and early '90s. ID is a technical label for a specific research project.

Carl: Did you read the Dover, PA, school board trial transcript in which Behe's testimony regarding "irreducible complexity" was crushed by a mountain of countervailing evidence? [2]

Jim: No, I haven't read the transcript, but I understand that the ID proponents claim that ID was not understood by the court, even though there was testimony by Behe, at least one credible ID proponent. He, so I understand, did not agree with the notion that ID should be taught in high school, for the very reason that it was not yet sufficiently established. Genuine ID advocates only want a place at the table of science. They may be Christians (and thus religious); as ordinary Christians they may advocate the biblical God as the designer they detect in their work in ID, but they do not argue for this in their technical papers.

Dawkins is much more prejudiced. He has no qualms about saying that evolution makes him a "fulfilled atheist." What's sauce for the goose is sauce for the gander, even though some geese (ID advocates) refuse to draw theological conclusions from scientific evidence. If they followed Dawkins, they could do so.

Carl: Did you read the judge's opinion in which he used the phrase "breathtaking inanity" to describe the intelligent design proponents' case?

---

[2] See Kenneth Miller, *Only a Theory* (New York: Penguin, 2008). For the judge's transcript see Relevant Readings, John E. Jones (p. 194). See also <www.pbs.org/wgbh/nova/id/>.

Jim: Did you know that the judge did not understand ID and that his opinion was written by the opponents of the school board? At least this is what some of my ID friends say.

Carl: The highly regarded Department of Biological Sciences at Lehigh University, in which Behe holds a position, has taken pains, in a written statement, to dissociate itself from him with respect to his positions on intelligent design and irreducible complexity. They do have standards.

Jim: Yes, standards that eliminate from the get-go any argument (even from scientifically accumulated data) that concludes that design is a better explanation of that data than the nondesigned mechanisms of *standard materialist science.* The deck is loaded. ID can't gain credibility under those circumstances. It's like a detective who concludes that his girlfriend has not "done it" and therefore never looks for any indication she did.

Carl: William Dembski, the "philosopher" of intelligent design has fared no better; his mathematical arguments have been discredited, and he has moved (with encouragement, I understand) from Baylor University to Southern Baptist Theological Seminary.

Jim: Dembski and his ID colleagues constantly work to respond to their critics. Are there some reasons that tell against ID? Then give the ID scientists the time to respond. ID scientists are aware that they are in for a long haul.

Did you know that Bill Dembski's major scholarly work on information theory, which is the background—so I understand—for his support for ID, is published by Cambridge University Press (*The Design Inference,* 2006); also see *Debating Design* (Cambridge University Press, 2004), a book edited by Dembski and Michael Ruse, an agnostic (maybe atheist) philosopher who treats ID with respect even though he disagrees with it.

I know Dembski and some of the other faculty of Baylor

personally—not well, but well enough to know that Dembski sealed his own fate when he was understood to claim a victory over the faculty objections to his appointment and to the institute he was establishing at Baylor under the auspices of the president (who did not have the confidence of the Baylor science faculty). The language in Dembski's email (or letter) was certainly misguided, or so I have been told by mutual friends. This put President Sloan in an awkward position, and he felt it best to distance himself from Dembski.

There was a tremendous amount of young arrogance and old-boy politics involved in Dembski's departure. Some (most?) of Baylor scientists had not given ID the chance to really develop; it was written off rather than refuted. The ID scientists only want the opportunity to present their case and to do the research that will either support their early hypotheses ("irreducible complexity," for example) or find them false or inadequate.

Galileo got shut out by the church. ID is being shut out by the church of scientism. Let the argument, let the research continue; let anyone who wants to know about it have access to as many sides of the argument as there are sides.

Carl: Please don't say you're tethered to the intelligent design mentality. Please. Please. Please.

Jim: Relax. I am an agnostic with regard to ID as a science or a philosophy (whichever it is). I don't know enough biology, nor do most of the people who are making declarations about how silly ID is. I'm willing to let the chips fall as they may. Let the ID story play out where it belongs——in the universities and the journals—not in the *New York Times* or the *New Yorker.* God created the universe; I do not know how.

Carl: My tether connects me to the natural world and the logic that flows from its workings.

Jim: I am tethered to the traditional Christian notion of a personal God who *created* a natural world in which ordinary natural science based on methodological naturalism can achieve an amazing amount of success, but cannot tell the whole story.[3]

Carl: In this world there is no evidence for ghosts and no need to invoke them—in fact, invoking them is a barrier to understanding. Take the tooth fairy, for example. I assume you've put that belief behind you because it wasn't supported by evidence, and you would agree that continued faith in this entity after reaching maturity is not healthy. I trust you've reached the same conclusion about Santa Claus, for the same reasons. Now follow this logic up the line through trolls, goblins, witches and their ilk to the hundreds of demigods and gods (such as Aphrodite, Poseidon, Apollo, Zeus and Wotan). All disposed of for lack of evidence. Only one more to go. C'mon, you can do it!

Jim: Surely you know that making a caricature of each other's views will get us nowhere. Why not add to your list of notions unworthy of belief just one more "myth"—naturalism? See why snide remarks put interesting arguments off point?

And while I am talking about red herrings and snide remarks, let me include the Flying Spaghetti Monster and the "Open Letter to Kansas School Board." Humor can disarm, but it can also obfuscate.[4]

So, all in good fun, I remain tethered to ordinary, traditional Christian theism, which, unlike you, I take to be *reasonable faith*. There are lots of reasons to think it's true, al-

---

[3] This does not mean that Jim believes that methodological naturalism is necessary for science. Good science may well be done within a framework of theistic naturalism (i.e., the notion that all so-called natural things and phenomena are ultimately dependent on God's sustaining presence and action; his direct action in nature must not be ruled out as out of bounds in scientific explanation).

[4] In an email not included in this collection, Carl had referred Jim to Dawkins's witty remarks about a Flying Spaghetti Monster. Google "Flying Spaghetti" and "Open Letter to Kansas School Board" for the background for this exchange.

ways have been. My own formal presentations in favor of the truth of Christian theism have been written for ordinary folk, not professional philosophers or scientists who venture into philosophy and theology. But I can put in your hand plenty of heavy-duty works presenting the case for Christianity for highly academic sorts of readers. Like me to do so?[5]

Jim

18

Unintelligent Design

Dear Jim:

Sorry for my snide remarks. I was just working on your monster email on "morality"[6] and had already apologized in that for prior flippancy. Thank you for teaching me the etiquette of debate.

My remark about Hume was in relation to his discussion of William Paley's "argument from design" based on his pocket-watch-in-the-woods model. I don't think it's too much of a stretch to connect that with the current ID movement. Regarding the latter, I understand, from reading some of Michael Behe's work, that the basis for ID is, at least in part, the supposedly irreducible complexity of biological systems such as the mechanism of blood clotting and the machinery of the bacterial flagellum. As was amply demonstrated at the Dover trial, no such irreducible complexity exists.

I must confess that I am dismayed that you are a devotee of the Discovery Institute. As I recall, this august body was

The wedge

---

[5] See Relevant Readings for books recommended by both Carl and Jim.
[6] Carl was referring to one of Jim's long emails, number nine in this book.

the brainchild of a super-Christian lawyer (the name, Phillip Johnson, comes to mind, but that could be wrong) after the failure of blatant creationism to infect our public school system. By eschewing direct association with religion, but promulgating the idea (with alleged proofs) that the workings of the world were so complex that they could only be the product of an intelligent designer beyond our ken, the IDers hope to create what they call a "wedge" issue that could be used to undermine the teaching of evolution and get ID into the classroom. With regard to Behe's comment that ID should not yet be taught in schools because it's not sufficiently established, he got that right. In fact, it's being decisively disestablished.

A threat to unfettered intellectual enquiry

What really bothers me about your position on this, Jim, is your failure to see not only the fundamental fallacy of the ID concept but also the threat it poses to unfettered intellectual enquiry. At what point in any investigation is it justifiable to conclude that the object of the investigation is the work of an intelligent designer?

Who is to make such a decision? What happens then? Do you halt the investigation and start praying? It would certainly seem like the logical thing to do. But no scientist worthy of the name (i.e., your "standard materialist scientist") could ever stop an investigation for any other reason than his not knowing how to proceed for the time being. His only valid position would be, "I don't know the answer—yet. I have to rethink my strategy." That's what keeps things moving ahead. Would a "nonmaterialist scientist" conclude that he'd reached the point of irreducible complexity, indicating ID at work? That sure would bring things to a dead stop. Is this the way you envision science operating?

Please don't lay any heavy-duty theological-philosophical texts on me. I can barely handle your simplified layman's version.

Well, back to your monster email.

Carl

19

Passionately Antireligious

Dear Jim:

Upon reviewing my responses to your email in the cold light of day, I realize that I did it again. I was gratuitously rude and offensive. I should have followed your example and presented my arguments with well-mannered conviction, but failed to do so. I confess that I am as passionately antireligious as you are religious, but I should have been able to maintain the level of decorum you exhibited. I do not retreat one iota from the substance of my arguments but regret that I did not present them in a less inflammatory manner. Please accept my apologies yet again. If we ever revisit this subject, I will do my utmost to convey my position in a more civilized manner.

Carl

20

Jim's Sabbath   A Dizzy Dream

Dear Carl:

If you needed to apologize (believe me at least this time!), apology accepted with delight!

I've been down with some minor malady associated with the urinary tract. No more details here. This has left me washed out, at times unable to trust myself driving my car. This morning I sat at my desk, feet up, and hallucinated going to my old office, which in the dream was being reconstructed. I got lost, became dizzy and would have collapsed had I not wakened. What triggered that? Probably reading that both of the medicines my doctor put me on yesterday to counteract whatever is making me ill can cause serious dizziness. Was I dizzy? Or did I dream it? How would I ever know? I don't think either science or religion is any help here.

Anyway, I am planning on putting aside for a few days any significant rejoinder to your more recent (and extensive) email. Let me say this, though: You have raised a number of issues I'm not as qualified to answer as I wish. We may be trying to take up too many at one time.

Cheers!

Jim

PART FIVE

OUR AGE

Sacred or Secular?

Fifty years ago, many intellectuals thought the whole world was abandoning religious belief and rapidly turning secular. Some Christian theologians, such as Harvey Cox in *The Secular City* (1965), not only agreed but argued that Christianity itself should become secular. Radical theologians, such as Thomas J. J. Altizer and William Hamilton in *Radical Theology and the Death of God* (1966), even proclaimed and gloried in the "death of God."

Today social scientists are the first to point out that this decline in religious belief and commitment has not happened. Christians of all persuasions have entered government and are visibly present in every social sphere. What does seem new is the recent spate of books by pundits, such as Richard Dawkins, Christopher Hitchens and Sam Harris, proclaiming atheism as the only scientific and intellectually respectable view.

Catholic scholar Robert Novak, in his essay "Remembering the Secular Age,"[1] responds to these charges, reasserting the vitality and intellectual sophistication of Christian Theism. He based his argument on a Princeton

---

[1] Robert Novak, "Remembering the Secular Age," *First Things*, June/July 2007, pp. 35-40.

survey that found "91 percent of Americans believe in God. Only 3 percent say they are atheists." Moreover, "87 percent of Americans identify with a specific religion, 2 percent Jewish, and 1 percent each Muslim, Buddhist and other." But not only do religious believers outnumber pure secularists, secularism itself has "significant incapacities," among them (1) a failure to provide a foundation for morality or to generate an ethic from its own intellectual base, (2) an inability to signal a purpose for humanity or an empathy for religious believers, (3) a lack of a standard by which to evaluate social progress, (4) "little to say about human suffering," (5) no response to terrorism, and (6) no reason to continue having "children in sufficient numbers to reproduce themselves." In fact, he concludes, "Atheism is not a rational alternative; it is a leap in the dark." Even agnosticism lacks the stamina to sustain human aspirations.

Science itself requires a firmer foundation than can be given by the autonomy of human reason. For, as Nietzsche pointed out more than a century ago, reason cannot ground reason; nihilism is the natural result of trying to do so. Novak concludes his essay with the practical values that religion provides and argues that, instead of giving up on religion because religionists often disagree with each other with violent results, all of us should learn to listen to and learn from each other: "To be forced to choose between science and religion, or between ways of reason and the ways of faith, is not an adequate human choice. Better it is to take part in a prolonged, intelligent, and respectful conversation across those outmoded ways of drawing lines."

21

Remembering Secularism

Dear Carl:

I just read the attached article on secularism by Robert Novak and could not figure out how to get the web address to you. So I downloaded it and am sending it as an attachment.

Novak's point of view is very close to mine.

Carl, I'm not sending this as a substitute for my own response to your latest missives. All in due course. All in due course. I've been pretty swamped this past week and, especially, weekend with the invasion of my grandchildren from Normal. Lovely kids, though.

I went to do exercises at the Wellness Center today, first time for a week. So I'm about back to my ordinary broken but functioning self.

Jim

22

Secularism Is Not Dead

Dear Jim and Phil:

Robert Novak is a very conservative Catholic and a member of the American Enterprise Institute. If you look at the membership roster of this august body, you will see that it consists of virtually all the neoconservatives that we have come to know and love over the last few years. The correspondence of Novak's religious views with yours is clear from the discussion we've already had (alas), but I would guess that you're politically and socially far more liberal than he is.

Phil, from the discussion we had last night, I would guess that you too might agree with Novak that Christianity is the fundamental (I use that term advisedly) moral foundation of our society. I don't agree with Novak, but I don't have the time or energy to wade through his article and attempt point-by-point rebuttals, especially since I have to leave for PA on Friday.

I will say, however, that his contention that we're just in the process of recovering from the ills of a secular interval seems a bit far-fetched, given the fact that by his estimate secularists comprise no more than 9 percent of the population. When has it been otherwise? Secularists seem to have power far beyond their meager numbers, according to Novak. Christians must man the battlements against the mighty avalanche of four books by Dawkins, Harris and Hitchens.

I find two sentences in Novak's essay (page 39, I think) particularly interesting and enlightening.

> Where atheism and agnosticism flourish one may find a certain moral carelessness seeping into common life, a certain slacking off, a certain habit of getting away with things.

This bald assertion is, as are the rest of his arguments, unsupported by evidence. In fact, you will remember, Jim, my reference to the article in the leading scientific journal *Nature,* which indicated that 93 percent of the members of the U.S. National Academy of Sciences are nonbelievers.[2] Would you agree that the leading scientists in America, if not the world, probably do not exhibit the moral slackness that the sentence quoted above would ascribe to them, despite the fact that atheism and agnosticism flourish in this population?

---

[2] Edward J. Larson and Larry Witham, "Leading Scientists Still Reject God," *Nature* 394 (1998): 313. See email exchange 6.

Secularism may be livable among specially gifted people but its effects on the less educated are less comforting.

Well, now we find out what Novak is made of. He is saying that the unwashed masses are not capable of handling secularism; it's only for the intellectual elite. So he would have no quarrel with my response to the first quoted sentence, but he's basically admitting that secularism is the province of higher intelligence. If secularism's so bad, why would 93 percent of the world's best minds be secularists? He's basically admitting that the only reason to promulgate the faith is to keep your average poor schlub happy, whereas smart folks don't need that crutch. There's your quintessential arrogant neoconservative in action.

Jim, I hope our continuing discussions will lead us away from this repellant viewpoint.

Carl

23

In Defense of Novak

For clarity and focus, Carl's comments on Novak are reprinted in sections with Jim's response following them.

Carl: Robert Novak is a very conservative Catholic and a member of the American Enterprise Institute. If you look at the membership roster of this august body you will see that it consists of virtually all the neoconservatives that we have come to know and love over the last few years. The correspondence of Novak's religious views with yours is clear from the discussion we've already had (alas), but I would guess that you're politically and socially far more liberal than he is.

Phil, from the discussion we had last night I would guess that you, too, might agree with Novak that Christianity is the fundamental (I use that term advisedly) moral foundation of our society. I don't agree with Novak, but I don't have the time or energy to wade through his article and attempt point-by-point rebuttals, especially since I have to leave for PA on Friday.

Jim: Yes, I am a bit more politically liberal than what I take Novak to be. I certainly would not try to justify the Iraq War with what I take to be Novak's take on it.

Carl: I will say, however, that his contention that we're just in the process of recovering from the ills of a secular inter-val seems a bit far-fetched, given the fact that by his estimate secularists comprise no more than 9 percent of the population. When has it been otherwise? Secularists seem to have power far beyond their meager numbers, according to Novak. Chris-tians must man the battlements against the mighty avalanche of four books by Dawkins, Harris and Hitchens.

Jim: Yes, I think Novak has overemphasized the secular-izing trends. The four books (I think it's now up to five or six aggressively atheistic books with the addition of Victor Stenger's *God: The Failed Hypothesis,* which I've dipped into but am not impressed with) are not going to have much lasting effect. Dawkins's *The God Delusion* has been panned by a lot of his atheist friends. Michael Ruse is embarrassed by it.

Carl: I find two sentences in Novak's essay (page 39, I think) particularly interesting and enlightening.

> Where atheism and agnosticism flourish one may find a certain moral carelessness seeping into common life, a certain slacking off, a certain habit of getting away with things.

This bald assertion is, as are the rest of his arguments, unsupported by evidence. In fact, you will remember, Jim, my reference to the article in the leading scientific journal *Nature,* which indicated that 93 percent of the members of the U.S. National Academy of Sciences are nonbelievers. Would you agree that the leading scientists in America, if not the world, probably do not exhibit the moral slackness that the quoted sentence would ascribe to them, despite the fact that atheism and agnosticism flourish in this population?

Jim: Atheists are a lot like Christians (i.e., they're human); some live better than they should, given their views; some live worse. I don't know how to count.

Carl:

Secularism may be livable among specially gifted people but its effects on the less educated are less comforting.

Well, now we find out what Novak is made of. He is saying that the unwashed masses are not capable of handling secularism; it's only for the intellectual elite. So he would have no quarrel with my response to the first quoted sentence, but he's basically admitting that secularism is the province of higher intelligence. If secularism's so bad, why would 93 percent of the world's best minds be secularists? He's basically admitting that the only reason to promulgate the faith is to keep your average poor schlub happy, whereas smart folks don't need that crutch. There's your quintessential arrogant neoconservative in action.

Jim: I don't believe Novak is "admitting" any such thing, but let that go for now. If Novak is doing that, I'm not. Besides, to be sure, there's enough arrogance going around for all of us.

Remember, Carl, my argument is not that atheists are bad people; many live lives better than those who proclaim to be Christian. My argument has always been that atheism has an inadequate foundation for morality. I hope sometime we can sit together and just go over that argument. I can't see why you don't see what I see. Maybe if we were to do that (without letting the conversation shift to lots of other things we disagree on), we could make some progress.

More later. I just hope (pray?) you find your time in PA helpful to Nancy and her mother.

Carl: Jim, I hope our continuing discussions will lead us away from this [Novak's] repellant viewpoint.

PART SIX

DOCTOROW

The Power of Doubt

Again the view of an outsider was inserted in the dialogue. A character in E. L. Doctorow's novel *The City of God* commented on the twin values of belief and doubt, which became another relevant focus for Carl and Jim. When Jim received the quotation from Doctorow, his first response was rather dismissive: "As you can imagine," he wrote, "there's not much in it with which I can agree." Eventually he became more attentive, and the dialogue continued.

24

A Highly Evolved and Beautifully Stated Religious Point of View

Dear Jim:

If you have to believe, this comment by Rabbi Sarah Blumen-thal, one of E. L. Doctorow's fictional characters, reveals a religious outlook that is about as good as it gets in my book.

> In the twentieth century about to end, the great civilizer on earth seems to have been doubt. Doubt, the constantly debated and flexible inner condition of theological un-certainty, the wish to believe in balance with rueful or nervous or grieving skepticism, seems to have held peo-ple in thrall to ethical behavior, while the true believ-ers, of whatever stamp, religious or religious-statist, have done the murdering. The impulse to excommunicate, to satanize, to eradicate, to ethnically cleanse, is a religious impulse. In the practice and politics of religion, God has always been a license to kill. But to hold in abeyance and irresolution any firm convictions of God, or an after-life with Him, warrants walking in His spirit, somehow. And among the doctrinaire religious I find I trust those who gravitate toward symbolic comfort rather than those who reaffirm historic guarantees. It is just those uneasy promulgators of traditional established religion who are not in lockstep with its customs and practices, or who are chafing under doctrinal pronouncements, or losing their congregations to charismatics and stadium-filling conversion performers, who are the professional reli-gious I trust, the faithful who read Scripture in the way Coleridge defined the act of reading poetry or fiction, i.e., with a "willing suspension of disbelief."

Yet they must be true to themselves and understand theirs is a compromised faith. Something more is required of them. Something more . . .

Suppose then that in the context of a hallowed secularism, the idea of God could be recognized as Something Evolving, as civilization has evolved—that God can be redefined, and recast, as the human race trains itself to a greater degree of metaphysical and scientific sophistication. With the understanding, in other words, that human history does show a pattern at least of progressively sophisticated metaphors. So that we pursue a teleology thus far that, in the universe as vast as the perceivable cosmos, and as infinitesimal as a subatomic particle, has given us only the one substantive indication of itself— that we, as human beings, live in moral consequence.

In this view the supreme authority is not God, who is sacramentalized, prayed to, pleaded with, portrayed, textualized, or given voice, choir, or temple walls, but God who is imperceptible, ineffable, except . . . for our evolved moral sense of ourselves.[1]

Carl

25

An Unbridgeable Gulf?

Dear Jim:

I forgot about your response to the Doctorow piece. I didn't

---

[1] E. L. Doctorow, *City of God* (New York: Random House, 2000), pp. 255-56.

agree fully with the piece because it still was at heart religious, but I was much taken with most of the point of view expressed. To struggle with honest doubt is to me far nobler than the unquestioning acceptance of traditional bromides. The degree to which you distance yourself from Doctorow's character's position reveals the gulf between us that I fear no amount of discussion will bridge.

Carl

26

Doctorow Reconsidered

Carl:
Okay. Let me be more thoughtful in my response to [Doctorow's Blumenthal].

> In the twentieth century about to end, the great civilizer on earth seems to have been doubt. Doubt, the constantly debated and flexible inner condition of theological uncertainty, the wish to believe in balance with rueful or nervous or grieving skepticism, seems to have held people in thrall to ethical behavior, while the true believers, of whatever stamp, religious or religious-statist, have done the murdering.

Jim: Doctorow's Blumenthal is utterly unfair. Doubt doesn't civilize; belief in and practice of what is truly moral and conducive to human flourishing civilizes. Doubt could only keep one from acting in any way at all. Passion for one's beliefs is not what makes believers dangerous. It's the content of their belief. Living in a community of passionate, even "fundamentalist," Quakers or other practicing pacifists would be quite safe, quite civilized.

Besides, it is not doubt that gets us where we'd like to be—in possession of the truth. It's discovering the truth either before or after one has doubted. Since we are creatures with both a finite and a broken intellect, doubt is indeed a part of the process of getting closer to the truth than we often get without it. But it must not be elevated to a principle above the notion that there is a truth to be found and for which we search. No scientists get much credit for shooting down an explanation. They make their reputation on proposing a more adequate solution to a tough question. Right?

The impulse to excommunicate, to satanize, to eradicate, to ethnically cleanse, is a religious impulse.

Jim: Okay, but only because it is first a generic human impulse.

In the practice and politics of religion, God has always been a license to kill.

Jim: Good grief! Of course not. Here is the fallacy of "hasty generalization." Where is the word "some"? Find the license for human beings to kill in the teachings of Jesus. Or, I think (I'm not sure), Buddha. Granted, you will find this in the Old Testament and in the Koran, but in both cases with considerable limit (not always as many as most of us would include today).

But to hold in abeyance and irresolution any firm convictions of God, or an afterlife with Him, warrants walking in His spirit, somehow. And among the doctrinaire religious I find I trust those who gravitate toward symbolic comfort rather than those who reaffirm historic guarantees. It is just those uneasy promulgators of traditional established religion who are not in lockstep

with its customs and practices, or who are chafing under
doctrinal pronouncements, or losing their congregations
to charismatics and stadium-filling conversion perform-
ers, who are the professional religious I trust, the faithful
who read Scripture in the way Coleridge defined the act
of reading poetry or fiction, i.e., with a "willing suspension of disbelief."

Jim: I think Coleridge did indeed intend the phrase "willing suspension of disbelief" to describe the "aesthetic distance" necessary for a reader's understanding and appreciation
of a work of the imagination—poetry or fiction. I don't think
he would have used it with a text of Scripture written with the
intention of conveying fact. Coleridge was, I gather, a rather
orthodox Christian, at least in his later years.

Yet they must be true to themselves and understand
theirs is a compromised faith. Something more is required of them. Something more . . .

Suppose then that in the context of a hallowed secularism, the idea of God could be recognized as Something Evolving, as civilization has evolved—that God
can be redefined, and recast, as the human race trains
itself to a greater degree of metaphysical and scientific
sophistication. With the understanding, in other words,
that human history does show a pattern at least of progressively sophisticated metaphors. So that we pursue
a teleology thus far that, in the universe as vast as the
perceivable cosmos, and as infinitesimal as a subatomic
particle, has given us only the one substantive indication of itself—that we, as human beings, live in moral
consequence.

In this view the supreme authority is not God, who
is sacramentalized, prayed to, pleaded with, portrayed,
textualized, or given voice, choir, or temple walls, but

God who is imperceptible, ineffable, except . . . for our evolved moral sense of ourselves.

Jim: Blumenthal's proposal is similar to that of physicist Paul Davies, who a few years ago won the Templeton Prize. See his *The Mind of God* or *God and the New Physics.*

Blumenthal does, of course, agree with me that there may well be (I'd say, is) a clear indication that there must be more to the universe and its foundation than matter in ordered motion.

I hope this clarifies my dissatisfaction with Blumenthal's position.

By the way, are all traditional bromides unwise or untrue? Did the ancients get nothing right? Lots of what passes as traditional wisdom was wise then and wise now, isn't it? Okay, question it, but don't reject it for being old. To do so is chronological snobbery, a rather nasty term for thinking that the latest is the bestest, so to speak. To put it in the terms of a recent bromide, "Don't believe anyone over thirty."[2]

Cheers!

Jim

27

Doctorow: Pro and Con

Again the emails flashed back and forth on the issue of doubt and certainty. Here's how a face-to-face dialogue would have gone.

Carl: I think Blumenthal, and maybe Doctorow himself, is

---

[2]Those who shouted this in the seventies are now, of course, well over thirty.

honestly searching for understanding and is skeptical of doctrinaire moral certitudes.

Jim: I agree. I don't doubt his honesty, just what he honestly believes.

Carl: Wherefore the doubt? He basically believes as you do; he's just not so cocksure about it.

The history of Christianity is soaked in blood as a consequence of the promulgation of such certitudes. As a Jew, whose forebears were slaughtered by the millions in the name of Christ down through the ages, he may have some justification for his position. Please don't say that those who performed these atrocious acts were not true Christians.

Christian certitude and the violence of history

You have only to read the works of Augustine, Aquinas and Luther to lay that to rest. In Nazi Germany the vast majority of Christians, including the churches, enthusiastically embraced Hitler (a self-proclaimed believer) and participated in the Holocaust. This is well documented in *Hitler's Willing Executioners* as well as in *Constantine's Sword,* which chronicles the earlier depredations against the Jews.[3] Pope John Paul visited Auschwitz to apologize for church-related crimes.

Jim: Why can't I say what is obvious? Inasmuch as self-acclaimed Christians violated the ethics of Jesus, of course they were not being true to the Christian faith as Jesus presented it. You admit that the pope disavowed the anti-Semitism of much of the church. Most Lutherans today would disavow the anti-Semitism of Luther. Put the blame where it belongs: on non-Christian behavior by self-confessed Christians.

Carl: You forgot Augustine and Aquinas. Given the magnitude of the crimes perpetrated by self-proclaimed Christians, it is self-evident that millions participated. Their belief did not alleviate their brutality. A Christian counterpart of

---

[3] James Carroll, *Constantine's Sword: The Church and the Jews* (Boston: Houghton Mifflin, 2001); and Daniel Jonah Goldhagen, *Hitler's Willing Executioners: Ordinary Germans and the Holocaust* (New York: Knopf, 1996).

Diogenes would have needed a megapowered lamp to find the minuscule number of Christians who were being true to the faith as Jesus presented it. Bully for the pope; his disavowal was a little late—par for the course for the church. I am putting the blame on non-Christian behavior by self-confessed Christians. That's the whole point. A lot of good their belief did them or their victims.[4]

Jim: I ignored Augustine and Aquinas because I am unaware of anything either of them taught that would justify the kind of violence perpetrated by, say, the Crusaders et al. Augustine, writing after Christianity had become a "state religion," wrote what is recognized as the first but most significant essay on "just war," which if it had been followed would have prevented most wars (World War II would be an exception). Just what of his or Aquinas's teachings did you have in mind?

Again, I don't deny that the violent Christians did what they did or that they thought they were justified in doing so. We agree that they were not justified in so believing and so doing. What they believed was wrong. They were doing what they believed. That was the problem. They ought not to have so believed. They were not in accord with the teachings of Jesus. End of case, for me at least.

Question: Why do you not mention the tremendous amount of good that Christians have done throughout the world? I am thinking primarily of medical service. In what country is there not a hospital called St. Luke's or St. Joseph's? Most of the AIDS relief has been done and inspired by card-carrying Christians, whether through specifically local or international religious-based institutions or through governments that have been urged by Christians to respond. Bono is a case in point. But their names are legion. Well, just a question.

---

[4]Carl got his information on Aquinas and Augustine from *Constantine's Sword,* pp. 305-6 and 334 (Aquinas), and pp. 146, 164, 315-19, 233, 270-71, 303, 446 (Augustine).

By the way, in response to the Holocaust, what about Corrie ten Boom (only one of many Dutch Christians who harbored Jews) or André Trocmé? (Check out these folk in Wikipedia.)

Carl: Christian moral certitude was also a dominant factor in such monstrosities as the Inquisition, the Crusades, the behavior of the Conquistadors, the enslavement of millions and the decimation of the Native Americans. Would that a modicum of uncertainty had stayed the hands of the perpetrators of these crimes, but justification for all these actions could be found in the Bible, so the devil take the hindmost. Recently Pope Benedict visited Latin America and acknowledged the church's ugly past, without actually apologizing, much to the frustration of the natives.

I know you will assert that Christianity is not to blame for any of this, but these acts were perpetrated by avowed Christians who affirmed their faith as justification for their actions. Why not believe them?

Jim: And why not believe their justifications were wrong? They may have thought they were justified by their Christian faith. But they were simply wrong about that. Read the Sermon on the Mount.

Carl: Again, the "they" to which you refer runs into the millions. Something's indeed wrong when so many think their monstrous deeds can be justified by their faith. Either the message didn't get through or the message is flawed in allowing such sick interpretation to poison the thinking of the vast majority of the faithful.

Returning to the idea of doubt or skepticism, it is essential to a scientific worldview. Why do you think Darwin reexamined his data for thirty years before publishing? His basic hypothesis has been upgraded to a theory by innumerable confirmatory observations, but it is still undergoing critical examination and modification. The observations of any scientist

Skepticism and science

are met with skepticism by other scientists, who immediately set out to prove him or her wrong. An unsupported proclamation of "truth" by a scientist would be viewed as having no merit. Scientists, by inclination and training, are skeptical about any unsupported assertions both in the scientific realm and in society at large. If this were more the norm, perhaps we wouldn't be in Iraq today. Perhaps you can don my moccasins and understand, at least a bit, why I am skeptical about the validity of the Bible and your passionately held moral certitudes about the existence of an omniscient, omnipotent and perfectly good God, given man's history and the current state of the world.

Jim: Of course skepticism plays a major role in any academic pursuit. All I was saying is that it does not play the primary role. The primary role is played by the active intellect and the imagination attempting to grasp the truth (of whatever the scholars are examining). Doubt comes after and adjusts the findings or rejects them. It just seemed to me that Doctorow's Blumenthal gave doubt an inordinate function. If Darwin had continued to doubt, his work would never have reached the public (unless his papers were found and someone else published them).

I think "humility" is a better way of describing the proper scientific and generally scholar attitude. Every scholar should be humble. Every scholar makes mistakes; no scholar wants to, but they do. It's quite appropriate for them to be skeptical about their own and others' work and yet go ahead and publish it, trusting that publication is better than silence. Nothing happens if one is so doubtful that no one's work gets aired and tested.

Carl: I don't have any serious quarrel with your remarks here, except that I don't think Blumenthal was being inordinately doubtful. She expresses skepticism about the validity of the "brass-band" type of worship and professions of faith and is more in tune with the idea of God as "the still small voice." I think this is a much more admirable religious stance, and I am surprised that you reject it.

28

Battling the Antitechnological Spirits

Dear Jim:

I'm totally ticked off. I just spent an hour responding to your response to my response, but I hit the wrong button and lost it all. Maybe it's God's judgment. I may try to work up the energy to recreate it, but family is starting to arrive for a big weekend here, and we'll be returning to Illinois toward the end of next week. So I'm not sure I'll be able to do any more of this for a while. I just wanted to let you know that I don't agree with your response to my response and had just about finished a devastating riposte (ha, ha), but I was thwarted by . . .

Hmm, I'm starting to get nervous.

Carl

29

Computers Don't Forgive

Dear Carl:

Ah! The spirits have begun their work. I don't get angry at my computer nearly as often as I have in the past. But what now bugs me most is when I hit a button that banishes my work into cyberhell. The problem is, my computer does what I tell it to, not what I want it to. Unlike God, my computer has no notion of forgiveness.

Anyway, not to worry. I still have at least two if not three of your emails to which I have yet to respond.

Enjoy your vacation from dialogue! And do take care on the interstates back!

Jim

30

Case Closed!

Dear Jim:

Another day has dawned, and I've decided to take up my poor splintered lance again. Of course, the quality of today's effort does not begin to match what God expunged from my computer yesterday. Evidently he shielded you from the annihilating power of those now lost words and has, moreover, addled my brain, preventing me from reproducing them. But I am compelled by my atheistic sense of morality to stagger back into the fray.

End of case?

I will address only one comment you made that really rocked me and addresses a fundamental difference between our worldviews. Your paragraph concerning the crimes of the Christians, which concluded with "End of case, for me at least," I find very disturbing (no. 27).

You glided, with what some might consider shamefully facile ease, past approximately two thousand years of the most monstrous behavior imaginable by millions of people who professed the same faith as you. Well, they were just wrong, you assert. Well, yes. Whole countries, whole societies, whole cultures were wrong but somehow believed utterly that they were acting as good Christians. I think the lesson here is the tremendous danger of their absolute certitude; it permitted them to commit unspeakable acts because they didn't have to examine the logic of their behavior; they had *faith.*

I think you should reconsider your dismissal of Blumenthal. Doctorow's fictional character understood the deadly potential of faith-based behavior. I can picture Doctorow [himself] confronting a frenzied mob of devout Christians bent on burning a heretic at the stake. "Hey folks, I'm a believer too, but are you absolutely sure this is the way to go? I'm really struggling with the issue of how God expects us to act toward nonbelievers."

The crowd's response? "Get lost, you wishy-washy equivocator. If you really, really believed, you'd just *know* what to do."

That seems to be what you think of Blumenthal too, although you really, really believe that the millions of really, really believing Christians who murdered and enslaved millions in the name of God were really, really not the good Christians they thought they were, even though they acted in good faith. From our discussions it seems apparent that you have no doubts whatsoever about the validity of your particular brand of Christian faith; it just differs from that of the murdering millions. But I think your mindset is just as dangerous.

Another disturbing aspect of your response is its apparent **Ho-hum!** ho-hum attitude: well, there were bad Christians, but that's an ocean of blood under the bridge, so let's dust those spatters off the gleaming cross and move on. As a moral atheist, I'm amazed at this cavalier attitude.

Shouldn't there be a major self-examination of the Christian belief system to understand how it could have engendered such criminality? Even though you personally have been a nice Christian, don't you feel the slightest discomfort at what has been perpetrated by a vast number of your fellow believers?

Is there something about the religion itself, or is it the possibility that the mechanism by which it is promulgated, i.e., through the fostering of unquestioning faith, that makes violent behavior easier?

If Christ were alive today, he would probably nail himself to the cross after seeing what has been done in his name. Do you think he would be satisfied with "Well, those Christians were just wrong. End of case, for me at least"? You owe him more than that glib brush-off.

Are Christians getting better? Maybe, in the last forty years out of their two-thousand-year history. I'll give you the benefit of the doubt on that, although international secular agencies for relieving world suffering have also been working to increasing effect. Meanwhile some old ways continue (e.g., the genocidal behavior of the Serbs and the covered-up sexual predation against children and others by the Christian clergy).

Abandon the smugness!

So, in sum, I think you (meaning all Christians) owe it to your religion to abandon the smugness associated with the knowledge that you are of the one true faith and instead engage in a deep examination of Christianity's overall effect on human society and whether any changes in its underlying principles and practices should be undertaken.

Well, I'm losing steam, although I'm still steamed emotionally, so I'll sign off.[5]

Carl

---

[5] Jim did not reply to this criticism of his smug attitude. He wishes he had. Readers may imagine that he would not wish his "case-closed" intellectual attitude to be read as implying he so easily washes the blood off his own hands or the hands of the historic Christian community to which he belongs. Its actions give it much for which to repent and sorrow over.

PART SEVEN

THE GOD QUESTION ONCE AGAIN

Carl and Jim don't agree on much, but they do agree on this: the question of both God's existence and his character is crucial to an intelligent and intelligible worldview. So once again Carl brings the subject back to issues that still hang in the balance.

31

Getting God Off the Hook

Carl remains unsatisfied with Jim's previous comments on why God created. So the informal debate continues with Carl commenting about where he is writing his responses (in Nancy's father's study in Pennsylvania) and complaining that one of his own email subject headings is coming back to haunt him.

Carl: Hey, could you please change the heading of your emails to something other than "Character Flaw"? I know I originated that heading in acknowledgment of my manifold defects, but having that continually come back at me is seriously undermining my self-esteem. It's bad enough that I have to sit here under a picture of a blue-eyed, very WASP-looking Jesus giving me the fisheye while I spout my heresies. I don't know if any defective character can survive the double onslaught of the eye of God and your impeccable arguments.

Jim: Okay, the subject heading is gone.

Carl: From what I can recall of your message, I don't think you can get God off the hook of responsibility so easily. You suggest that God's creation of man was not out of necessity (no. 14), but from some lighter emotion, such as a creative urge equivalent to painting or photography (how about musical composition?). We could argue about that, but the fact remains that God purposely created beings (including angels) that could and did get into trouble big time. He didn't have to do that. He could have created beings that would never be able to do bad things. Why didn't he do that?

The obvious answer is that it would have been a completely useless exercise, so he had to include the potential for evil in the creation. In doing this he knew what would happen;

Why did God create beings who could commit so much evil?

much suffering would ensue. If you argue that he wanted all his creatures to freely love him, thereby avoiding evil, you have to ask, what if they all did and freely chose never to visit the dark side? Well, then he would be in the same position that would have obtained if he had made creatures incapable of doing bad things. Again, what would be the point of the whole exercise? Unless you want to completely abdicate your "God-given" capacity for rational thought, you have to conclude that God knowingly brought evil into existence because he had to in order to make the flow of history that we're now a part of possible.

Jim: My comment about God's "need" to do what he did in creation was not to suggest that photography is equivalent to creating human beings, only to show that we do all kinds of things we don't need to do. If we can do this rationally, so can God.

Perhaps God wanted to share his "personal" (self-understanding and self-determination) freedom with a creation? Perhaps he knew that the results, as much as they involved our and his own suffering, would far surpass the intensity and scope of that suffering. Perhaps he had a host of reasons for creating, reasons that we simply can't guess—or even imagine. Remember, God really is omniscient; he really is omnipotent; he really is good. And he really is beyond our attempts to second-guess. Perhaps, perhaps, perhaps. These perhapses are just as rational as your suggestion that he "needed" to do what he did and by doing it showed that he was incompetent and unworthy to be anything we would want to call a God.

The mystery of God   That there is a tremendous mystery about an omniscient, omnipotent, omnipresent, good God is not an unreasonable notion. We know of a host of creatures who live in the ocean, but we have only recently come to learn about the further host that lives near the bottom of the deepest seas. We don't know what we don't know. There may be creatures we will never know about. There may well be some things about these known creatures that we not only don't know but that we can't know. We can't know what we can't know, unless someone who knows (God, for example) tells us. So we can hardly charge God with stupidity, ineptness, bad faith and evil based on what we think we know now. Nonetheless, in the life, teachings, death and resurrection of the incarnate Son of God, we have a wide window into the character of a God whose love and compassion, teamed with his faultless sense of righteousness, show him worthy of worship.

Carl: I know most of my arguments are going to bounce right off you, just as yours do off me. I think this fact gives me the edge, though. It supports my contention that our brains are wired differently. Some people need religion, others don't. Religious and nonreligious people can be either mostly good or mostly bad (nobody's completely one or the other). I would argue that those who are mostly good without recourse to religion have a leg up. I wonder, if you lost your religion, do you think you would turn mostly bad? Is it belief in God that's keeping you from becoming a ravening beast?

Brains wired differently

Jim: Do you really want to talk about our different religious sensitivities as being due to different "wiring"? Once one heads down this road, materialistic determinism takes over. It keeps both of us from being "rational." All our doubts and beliefs, all our ignorance and knowledge, are then "caused" by factors over which we have no control. If we do have control over our thoughts and conclusions, we have a freedom that may use "wiring" but must not be determined by "wiring." Nihilism (both ethical and intellectual) is never far from pure naturalism.

What would I do if I lost my faith? Who knows? I don't. But from where I stand now, I would guess that I would become a hedonistic nihilist. I would probably continue to be about as "good" as I now am, but I would do so from encul-

If I lost my faith . . .

turation, habit and the judgment that being "good" would make me happier (here's the hedonism) than living solely for the satisfaction of my basest desires (money, sex and power). If Christian theism is not true, some form of nihilism is the most rational alternative. When naturalism tries to explain (1) the existence of goodness, (2) the existence of human free will, or (3) the reason a purely natural mind can be justified in believing that it can reach the truth about anything (material or spiritual), its explanations are utterly inadequate. Better be a nihilist. It's more honest.

God— certifiably insane?

Carl: On the subject of nonbelievers, I had a very brief talk with Nancy's brother the other day. He's the professor with the PhD in religious studies from Temple and has analyzed the Bible in minute detail. I fear this will annoy you, but he has concluded that the God portrayed in the Bible is certifiably insane. I know, I know, you think that's an extreme atheistic position, but he's really a nice guy and seems to have a pretty strong scholarly background in the area in question.

Jim: Of course your brother-in-law's position is a form of "extreme atheism." Do most atheists reach this conclusion? But "extreme" is not necessarily either true or false, and it's truth and falsity that matters. By the way, being "nice" is no test of whether the one who is "nice" is correct. There are lots of nice people around. Hey! You're a nice person. I'll let you judge whether I am.

But is God insane? Well, some of Jesus' contemporaries thought he was insane. And there is that trilemma that C. S. Lewis posed (as others before him): Given how Jesus is presented in the Gospels and assuming that it is a fairly accurate picture, he must either be a liar, a lunatic or the Lord himself. So maybe one could say this of God. It's a thought.

Extreme atheism

Carl: Also relevant is the web address provided in one of your emails. I looked it up, and it turned out to be an interview of some Oxford don by a representative of the Templeton

Foundation. The interviewer kept trying to get the Oxford guy to acknowledge that there was some kind of intelligence behind evolution. The interviewee kept agreeing that there is the appearance of intelligence because random mutations provide a plethora of variants and the survival of the most fit variants for a given environment looks like an intelligent selection process. After several attempts by the Templeton guy to get him to agree that it actually *was* an intelligent process, the Oxford guy finally said, "Look, I'd better lay my cards on the table; I'm an atheist."

Me too.

Jim: Well, here is something we can agree on. A prior commitment to atheism will always be a barrier to an openness to consider whether theism is untrue. Walk a mile in one's opponent's moccasins. It can be done, but only with courage and great passion for the truth.

Now, whether the biological world presents enough evidence to make the notion of design a rational conclusion, I don't know. Let the scientists who actually look at the evidence look and see, or look and hesitate, or look and not see. This sort of science (ID) is just beginning.

32

A Colloquy on the God Hypothesis

Again the emails crossed back and forth. Two emails are combined here. Together they show the flow of question and answer, charge and countercharge.

Carl: I really don't think you're being fair in laying down the ground rules for this discussion. If I have to accept your asser-

Who makes the rules?

tion that God is omniscient, omnipotent and perfectly good, and that the Bible is his inerrant word as the starting point, then the discussion is over. If I try to use logic to counter your assertions, you say that God and his machinations are unknowable, except via revelation, and my arguments are mere speculation. Talk about walking in another's moccasins! I've done nothing but walk in yours!

Jim: It's my turn now to apologize. If I've not been walking in your moccasins (at least sometimes), it's not because I haven't tried. I believe it's important to see every argument from two standpoints: (1) the standpoint of the one who is making it and (2) one's own standpoint. Understanding comes first, then critique. I'm sorry to have failed. I'll try harder.

Actually I think you've generally done a good job walking in my shoes. So on to my response and my attempt at least to understand your point of view.

The unnecessary God hypothesis

Carl: From my standpoint, the God hypothesis is completely unnecessary to explain anything that goes on in the universe. Most scientists would agree with that assessment.

Jim: Yes, I understand where you stand. I hesitate to agree that the extent of those who side with you with what I take to be such certainty (of atheism) is so large. But I am confident that there is not such a preponderance of atheism among scientists.

How many scientists are atheists?

Without anything but experience and anecdotal evidence to go on at this time, here is how I think their beliefs or nonbeliefs would break down:

- atheist (Richard Dawkins, Carl Sagan, Victor Stenger): 10-15 percent

- agnostic due to skepticism or lack of interest in the issue (many of these scientists do not reveal their beliefs about God; perhaps Stephen Jay Gould, who thinks the methodology of science has nothing to say about metaphysical issues [whether there is more to the universe than matter, for example]): 50 percent

- belief in some sort of transcendent or immanent-transcendent, e.g., a "mind" in the universe (e.g., Paul Davies, Fritjov Capra, Lewis Thomas): 15 percent

- specifically theistic (Muslims, the religiously Jewish, Christian; e.g., Francis Collins, Owen Gingrich): 20-25 percent

Granted, I don't have any statistical studies to back this up. But I'm fairly certain that even in the academic community there is a preponderance of belief that there is some kind of spiritual dimension or at least could be. Outright doctrinaire atheism (Dawkins) is not, I would imagine, preponderant even among scientists in the National Academy of Science. I know, the figure you and others cite is 93-percent atheist, but I'd bet that figure includes a very large number of agnostics or those who don't seem to care. No need to challenge me on these figures. I know they're guesses. I'm on the lookout for well-conducted polls.[1] But very little can be made of percentages of belief anyway. Everyone could be wrong.

Carl: If you read Gould's book *Wonderful Life,* about the soft-bodied sea-dwelling organisms that populated the earth 540 million years ago (fortuitously preserved in the Burgess Shale in Canada), you will see that he concluded that the appearance of vertebrates, including man, was contingent on the emergence and survival of a small, insignificant creature (*pikaia gracilis* is the approximate spelling, I think) with a rudimentary backbone. Gould contended that if the evolution-

---

[1] Jim was obviously having difficulty in accepting that so many elite scientists were atheists, but Carl was insistent. Alister McGrath and Joanna Collicut McGrath cite and comment on two polls years apart (one as recent as 1997) that show that some 40 percent of scientists believe in a God to whom one can pray and expect to receive an answer. See their *The Dawkins Delusion? Atheist Fundamentalism and Denial of the Divine* (Downers Grove, Ill.: Inter-Varsity Press, 2007), pp. 42-43.

ary tape was replayed from the beginning, the overwhelming probability is that such an organism would never have developed, and mankind (and consequently metaphysics) would never have arisen. Gould's interpretation of the evolutionary data was that contingency ruled, i.e., the whole process was completely random and not directed by a higher intelligence. If the very existence of man is a "lucky" toss of the dice, as Gould contends, then so are any man-made metaphysical considerations about "whether there is more to the universe than matter, for example." (Kind of hard to fit the biblical story of the creation in here, don't you think?) Gould was not a believer. His NOMA [nonoverlapping magisteria] idea was an attempt to defuse what he perceived as the hostility between science and religion by declaring them to be mutually exclusive and mutually nonthreatening ways of looking at the world. Who am I to disagree with him about NOMA? (But I tremblingly and respectfully do, I'm afraid.)

Natural humanity   I think this is a good place to reiterate my overall position. I agree with Gould and other students of evolution that man arose via random mutation and natural selection (i.e., the ability of a given mutant form to survive and reproduce in the environment in which it finds itself). He is no different from any other species in this regard. There is nothing to distinguish him from any other organism except the size and complexity of his brain (again, the product of mutation and selection).

It is abundantly clear, with absolutely no evidence to the contrary, that all of man's qualities depend on the physical integrity of his brain. Thus, there is no evidence for a "ghost in the machine," no homunculus in the pineal gland, soul or any other supraphysical component that is the source of man's behavior. Likewise, evolution does not require the participation of a nonmaterial designer; it works just fine without the invoking of divine intervention.

So, if we're completely physical beings just like all other

species, what about free will? Well, it's no more necessary or sensible to invoke such a supraphysical attribute for man than it is for any other animal. Being strictly physical entities comprised of hardware (our genetically programmed bodies) and software (the information our brains have accumulated), the manner in which we interact with our environment at any given instant is determined by the interplay of these two aspects of our being, just as in other animals.

Of course, we are constantly changing as we continually learn from experience (obviously much more than animals with simpler brains), but each of us processes the incoming information somewhat differently, owing to our genetic differences. All this smacks of determinism, which it is in a sense, but if you read a couple of books on chaos theory and fractal geometry, you would see that the imponderables affecting each situation are so vast (e.g., a butterfly flapping its wings in Calcutta affecting the weather to the extent that a hurricane appears off the Louisiana coast) that the consequences of one's actions are impossible to predict. Quantum theory also introduces an element of unpredictability into each event.

I emphasize that no spirituality of any kind is required to explain any aspect of our existence. Although you invoke the necessity for such spirituality to engender morality and the other higher human attributes, this reasoning is specious. Such attributes are emergent characteristics of the complex human brain and are present in less sophisticated form in animals with brains that are fairly complex but less so than ours.

The rest is mythology to fill in temporary gaps in our knowledge and bring psychological comfort to those who fear the unknown and the death that awaits us all. That's the end of the argument for me. But I've put that aside and attempted to understand the religious point of view, admittedly without abandoning the logic that informs my scientific outlook. You, on the other hand, have not even put on my moccasins, let alone walked in them. If you did so, you would have to subject the God hypothesis to some logical analysis. Let's explore the following example.

Jim: Okay. Let's.

Carl: From everything you've said I believe, you can safely assert that God made man with the free-will capacity to be perfectly good or perfectly evil, with all possible shadings between these two extremes. As I understand your assertion, God is fully pleased when man is perfectly good and displeased when man strays from this ideal. Now, in all fairness you have to allow God to give man the capacity to be perfectly good. If you say that man by nature is imperfect and unable to fully please God, then the sin would be God's for creating a being constitutionally unable to perfectly please him. So now man is faced with a free-will choice, and it is entirely possible that he would unerringly choose to be perfectly good.

This is not speculation; it follows logically from the God hypothesis that you espouse. On this basis it is entirely possible that the first humans God created would have unhesitatingly eschewed temptation and freely chosen to remain in Eden and worship at the feet of God. As I understand the creation story, they would have never died and been eternally happy in God's presence, freely following his wishes down to the last jot and tittle. God would never have cause to become angry or anguished, and punishment would be nonexistent. Again, I don't think it would be fair of you to dismiss this situation as mere speculation. From everything you've said about God, it is what he desires, and there's no reason why it couldn't happen.

Jim: Yes, with one sidebar, this is, I think a fair way to put it. The Eastern Orthodox theologians believe that if Adam and Eve had not sinned, they might well have died physically and been resurrected to eternal life, but history would have continued through their progeny. Remember, prior to their rebellion they were asked to multiply and fill and tend the earth (Genesis 1:28).[2] But over the course of centuries, humankind would have grown in spiritual discernment and been perfected (from, as it were, good seed). The Orthodox call this process *divinization,* though they do not mean by it that they would become gods. Rather, they would become like the incarnate Son of God. The incarnation would have happened even if humankind had not needed a savior to suffer and die for their rebellion, but the crucifixion would not have happened.

C. S. Lewis sets his science-fiction novel *Perelandra* on Venus, where the first human-like couple are tempted but do not rebel. It's an interesting story. Give it a read if you're not familiar with it.

In any case, your question has been dealt with both in profound Christian theology and imaginative fiction.

Carl: "Imaginative fiction" is the operative phrase here. I think my moccasins fell off during this part of your discussion. The logic escapes me. Here we have a perfectly good God who in his perfection would presumably be perfectly happy. This is evidently not the ideal state, however, because he would have nothing to do. (I think monopolarity is creeping in here again.) So, out of a desire to create even more than the perfect level of happiness that now obtains, he creates lesser beings that, despite their best efforts, can never attain the level of happiness that he enjoys. And this is only if they don't fall into the temptation trap he prepared for them. (God, what a helluva guy!)

Divinization as imaginative fiction

The logic problem here is that while the realization of God's plan might increase the *quantity* of happiness in his domain (more happy entities besides himself), the overall *quality* of happiness in heaven would be diminished because of the dilution effect produced by the necessarily inferior happiness

---

[2] This addresses Carl's suggestion below that perhaps Adam and Eve would not have had progeny had they not sinned.

of the lesser beings. The same problem would seem to exist for goodness and any other attribute you wish to consider. So the question again arises: What's God getting out of this?

What does God get out of creation?

The question is not only based on the dilution problem just cited but also on the fact that the perfectly good creatures that never sinned or had to overcome trials and tribulations (not fair of God to dump such things on them now, after they've been so good) would have no body of experience from which to learn and grow. They would all have to be educated by God or by some other heavenly experience (the divinization process?).

So what's the payoff for God? Would he be able to hold stimulating conversations with his little buddies on heavenly affairs? What insights would they bring to the table? Whatever they could offer, it would invariably be inferior to his level of understanding. My moccasins tell me that God would end up with a horde of utterly boring lesser copies of himself. Maybe he would just observe them without interacting. But wouldn't that be akin to our watching a colony of hamsters? It's fun for a while, but for all eternity?

Okay, everything God desired has come to pass; free will worked exactly as he had hoped, and the Garden of Eden is populated by perfectly worshipful beings who had by free choice never strayed from adherence to his goodness from the very moment he created them. Now I ask you to put on my moccasins and ask yourself what God could possibly get out of such an exercise. And what would his creatures get out of it (besides a continual orgasm of joy, of course)? No hiding behind God's inscrutability. Please enlighten me.

The joy and glory of sharing joy

Jim: Since the Bible is largely silent in answer to your question, any suggestion I make is highly speculative. But let me try.

God might well get joy out of the joy his creatures receive. We get joy out of seeing our children enjoying their play, seeing our friends enjoy an afternoon at the zoo or an evening at the Chicago Symphony Orchestra, even seeing total strangers enjoying watching the Cubs win. Maybe God made us in his image in part in order to share his own interpersonal joy (within the Trinity) with the mutually shared joy of others with each other and others with himself. Thus he would be creating out of his generosity.

Carl: Your analogy doesn't work. We get joy from the children we have produced because we know they have the potential, if properly nurtured, to surpass us and contribute more to society and life in general than we did. We get joy from other humans whose qualities we admire and might wish to emulate. God's attitude toward us is much less laudable; it is akin to what we feel for our pets, benign but unavoidably condescending because he can never experience the joy we get from fostering the development of beings that can accomplish more than we did.

Jim: The apostle Paul had a lot to say about joy in his letter to the Philippians. Here's one bit:

> For to me, to live is Christ and to die is gain. If I am to go on living in the body, this will mean fruitful labor for me. Yet what shall I choose? I do not know! I am torn between the two: I desire to depart and be with Christ, which is better by far; but it is more necessary for you that I remain in the body. Convinced of this, I know that I will remain, and I will continue with all of you for your progress and joy in the faith, so that through my being with you again your joy in Christ Jesus will overflow on account of me. (Philippians 1:21-26 NIV)

Wouldn't receiving such joy be a sufficient reason for his creating us? Maybe there's more to joy than meets our understanding. Heaven seems to be full of it. It does look like joy is a pretty good deal, especially when you see that it is linked it to interpersonal relationships between parents and children,

Handel in every language

parents with each other and all of the family with all of the rest of the family.

Today our families experience joy not just within the limits of our finitude but within the limits of our brokenness as well. What if the brokenness were to be healed and we would be restored to full image-of-Godness?

Think of it—human beings constituted to the full extent of likeness to God (who is personal, social [trinitarian], righteous, good and loving)! Wouldn't such a creator God be worthy of worship? Would not obedience to this God be a joy? Wouldn't such worship itself be a joy? My wife and I, too, are thrilled at the joyful worship of Handel's *Messiah*. Imagine it being sung in every different language and all be understood by all, either because each of us understood every different language or heard every different language as if it were our own?

Of course the *Messiah* is an oratorio that would not have been written if Adam and Eve had not rebelled. So the real story with which we have to deal is not what would have happened if they had not sinned but what happened because they did.

Carl: As I suggested above, the joy of obedience to God is akin to the joy experienced by a lap dog in obeying his master. It does not begin to match the joy we can experience in our relationships with our children or with other humans for which we have affection and respect.

Knowing good and evil [What about the] full implications of God's first creatures' free-will decision to heed his warning and not to give in to temptation? It's interesting that the nature of this temptation was the fruit of the tree of the knowledge of good and evil. In turning away from the consumption of this fruit, Adam and Eve would perforce be denied this knowledge and would thus be as innocent babes at the feet of God. It doesn't seem clear whether or not they would procreate under these circumstances. In any case, I will be interested to hear your take on God's reaction to the realization of his stated wishes.

Jim: The only one in the Genesis account who says that
eating the fruit of the knowledge of good and evil will bring
Adam and Eve to the knowledge of what is both "good" and
"evil" is the serpent. Adam and Eve knew what was good before they ate the fruit: what was good was to obey God. (After
all, God is utterly good; what he commands must be within
the framework of that goodness. Moreover, granting his goodness, it must have been good for God to give them the choice
to eat or not eat. Adam and Eve were innocent, not because
they had no knowledge at all of good and evil, but because
while they knew good both intellectually and experientially,
they knew evil only intellectually. It's the difference between
knowing what adultery is and becoming an adulterer.)

So, to repeat, Adam and Eve knew *intellectually* what it was
to be good (obey) and evil (disobey). When they ate the fruit,
they came to know evil by *experience;* that is, they became
associated with evil; they became evil's first human perpetrators. This, then, broke their intimate relationship with God
and led to their own broken relationship and that of their family. Likewise it led to the misunderstanding of good and evil
by them, their progeny and the progeny's progeny.

Except for God's redemptive action in history, his gradual
revelation of himself through the Hebrew people and finally
through the incarnate Son of God, we would be far more con-
fused about what is good and not good than we are today. The
historical foundation of today's Western secular *humanist* ethics is to be found primarily in the Old and New Testaments
(not the Greeks, not the Egyptians, not Confucius, not the
Buddhists, not the Hindus, not the primal religions).

The foundation of Western ethics

Yes, there is progress in the understanding of the ethical
dimension. War may be justified in Old Testament terms but
hardly in terms of the New. Yet the New builds on the Old
and can't be well understood without understanding the Old.

Perhaps there is no such thing as Judeo-Christianity as such, but most of the values of, say, the *Humanist Manifesto* are the same as those of the New Testament (though without its transcendent foundation). The Enlightenment values so cherished today by humanists are the remainder of a truncated Christian faith; they are what is left when God is no longer thought to be necessary or even to exist.

Carl: Well, you got off the track here. I had asked what you thought God's reaction would be to being adored by really good simpletons who had no knowledge of good and evil. You got us back into original sin and the sacrifice of the incarnate son of God. I don't want to go over all that again. I do have to disagree with your bald assertion that none of the civilizations preceding the advent of Christianity matched the latter in ethical and moral understanding. As I've said in previous discussions, the ethical and moral precepts espoused by Christianity are basic to the survival of any human society, including those non-Christian ones that managed to eke out reasonably splendid social and intellectual existences for two to three thousand years before Christ.

33

The Scandal of the Particular

This dialogue contains the contents of three emails, written earlier. The first two paragraphs are from chapter 15. Carl initiates the topic: the similarities and differences among the world religions.

Carl: You know how all the other religions are man-made myths that arose at different times in our history? How come the one true religion resembles all the other mythical ones in this respect? It seemed to appear in some scraggly desert tribe at some given point in time. Did the one true God finally decide that it was time he made an appearance? Why did he allow so much time to elapse, during which myriad other false gods and religions were concocted?

A logically defensible as well as a morally upright God would have been in man's consciousness from the beginning. The gods of the Egyptians, Greeks, Romans, Sumerians, etc., were obviously made up in good faith to satisfy man's need to fill gaps in our understanding of the natural world. Why did God allow man to be clueless for so long when he didn't have to? The whole thing looks pretty suspicious to me. The fact that the one true God emerged in the same manner as all the other false gods suggests that he may actually be in the same category as the other deities, i.e., a gap-filling myth.

Jim: Yep! You got it. This classic objection is called the "scandal of the particular." It has often been raised by critics and skeptics. The answer that I think fits best is this: we really don't know why.

I know you don't like me to raise the argument from the "inscrutability of God," but I do it boldly. The idea that God can be totally understood from a human standpoint is unreasonable. How dare we think that God has to fit our notion of what he should be! Read the last few chapters of the book of Job.

Carl: How dare we? Because God gave us a brain that is designed to figure things out logically. The dictionary defines faith as belief that is not supported by logic or evidence. To me, the practice of faith is a perversion of God's design (walking in your moccasins). What I get from your remarks is that God prefers, and may even demand, an allegiance to him based on faith rather than informed understanding (how dare we think we can understand!), thus attributing to him base qualities more suitable to an egotistical human dictator. Unfortunately, this view of God is supported by his execrable behavior in the book of Job. God gives you an analytical brain and is angry when it functions as expected, a clear sign of dementia.

Jim: I am not throwing my brain out of the window when I say this. I am delighted to use reason to guide, even to critique, faith. I do not reject doubt as a tool.

Carl: Really? It's news to me. In all our discussions the basis for the logic you profess always starts from the premise that God exists in his perfect goodness and can do no wrong. This is pure faith. I have read no critique of this position from you.

Jim: But I want to recognize that there are necessarily some things none of us humans will be able to understand. The question is, in the longest run, which story—that of Christian theism, naturalism (atheism), pantheism, etc.—best fits the way we experience the whole scope of reality. The whole of the Christian worldview should be pitted against the whole of other worldviews. I've done this in simplified form in *The Universe Next Door.* That book makes a better response to your questions than the piecemeal approach of our current dialogue. If Christianity has questions yet to be answered, so do the alternatives.

God has been vastly generous in what he has told us of himself, his nature and his desires. Most of this is something we could never have imagined. If God really is like he says he is in Scripture, we could never have figured it out for ourselves.

Carl: How true! A logical mind (not insulated by faith) reading the Bible reaches the conclusion that God is a malignant entity, with all the attributes of a very disturbed human being.

Jim: But he didn't answer all the questions we might ask. Rather, he answered the most important ones and has given us the ability to grasp these answers with enough clarity and certainty to give our lives back to him and to seek to live in his will.

Carl: Only if you rely on faith rather than reason. By the way, it's interesting that you often sound like a preacher ("seek to live in his will"). This phraseology crops up so often in your writing; I think you missed your calling.

Jim: If God were only what we could and have imagined, we would think him a very different sort of God. Every religion other than the classical theistic ones (Judaism, Christianity and Islam) are basically pantheistic (one God [Brahman as in Advaita Vedanta Hinduism, or many gods as in primal religions]). That is, the divine and the material are somehow and finally one. The human imagination tends to gravitate toward some form of pantheism. One could say that one indication that the Christian worldview came from God is that it is the sort of view, the sort of story, that no human being, society or culture could imagine on his or her or its own.

Carl: Fascinating! You're expressing exactly why I think the Christian worldview is inferior to those tending toward pantheism. You agree that to the human mind, provided by God, the merging of the divine with the material universe makes more sense than the Christian view, which you have to accept purely on faith. But to you, the fact that you have to negate or suppress your God-given logical faculties in order to entertain the Christian worldview validates that worldview. Boy, you Christians are a caution!

Jim: Theism alone talks of a God who creates *ex nihilo*. He brings into being something that had not previously existed. Natural history begins with that creation. The universe is not made out of him or it, but is willed into being.

Of course there would be no way of knowing that this is the case if it were not revealed to us. Other religions speak of enlightenment; that is, a human self comes to realize its/his/her own divinity and speaks from that self-realization. Theistic religions alone speak of direct revelation from one personal God to people (prophets). In other words, theists claim that the true story of our origin, purpose and destiny comes from God.

Carl: Direct revelation. What's that? I seem to have been denied it somehow. Hey, God, here I am! Oh, I have to shut down my logic circuits? Sorry, the surrender of my intellectual integrity is too high a price.

Jim: Second, in Christian theism the salvation of humankind—if it comes—comes by grace (a direct gift from God). Reconciliation with God is a gift. Eternal life is a gift. It is not earned. This is a key emphasis of Christianity that separates it from both Islam and Judaism. When people imagine their religion, their solution to humankind's deadly weaknesses, they almost always imagine human beings saving themselves by their own actions.

Only the theistic religions emphasize history. God created. Humans rebelled. God did what was necessary to reconcile them to himself. What happened to enact this happened not in an abstract "ideal realm" but on Earth. In the beginning, there was one couple. God chose one man—Abraham—and his progeny to be the person and people through whom he would gradually reveal himself. Finally God the Son became one man at one time and at one place. Christianity especially is a very particular religion. But it is a religion that the incarnate Christ told his disciples to spread throughout the world. Heaven is seen as a place where people of every tongue and nation celebrate God's amazing grace together. The particular becomes very large indeed.

Christians embrace the scandal of the particular; it is only a scandal to those who do not see the truth it embodies.

Carl: The above is just a reiteration of the same old platitudes, couched in the same old religious jargon with which we began our whole interchange. If you rest your worldview on the foundation of faith rather than evidence and the logical interpretation of evidence, what you call "truth" comes across as a lot of mystical gibberish. You claim to delight in using reason to guide faith, but you're really using faith to guide reason, which has the effect of completely negating reason. Nowhere have I seen you critique your faith or use doubt as a tool, as you claim to do.

34

A Believer's Crutch

One email from Carl seems to have escaped any response from Jim. In the editorial process, Jim thought it odd but intriguing. Moreover he couldn't help giving a brief rejoinder. And Carl could not help but reply.

Carl: On the basis of our discussions to date, I think we can agree that an atheist who's a paragon of goodness and a Christian with the same superlative qualities would, on the basis of their actions, be indistinguishable to an observer who was unaware of their disparate views on religion. This equivalence of character raises an interesting issue.

When I asked you what would happen to you if you lost your faith, your answer seemed to indicate that you would be somewhat diminished. If this is true of believers in general, it is reasonable to conclude that they are disadvantaged when compared to atheists of equivalent goodness.

Evidently, believers need the crutch provided by their faith to reach their maximum level of goodness, while atheists require no such aid. As far as I can see, the only counterargument you can mount against this conclusion is that believers are always at a higher level of goodness than atheists. Although no studies have been done to test such a premise, I don't believe that any reasonable person would support it. However, I'm sure you will come up with a better refutation of my conclusion.

Jim: The argument has a hidden premise, to wit, that a person with a false view of reality who also behaves well by human standards can somehow be morally equivalent to a person with a true view of reality who also behaves well by human standards. But there are at least two major problems with this argument.

First, either the Christian or the atheist holds a false view of reality. If it is the Christian who is wrong, he or she still can be highly moral by human standards. But if it is the atheist who is wrong, he or she will not be ranked by human standards but by God's standards, which include such enjoinders as loving your enemy or allowing yourself to be cheated or used by others (see the Sermon on the Mount [Matthew 5—7]). Surely being moral means having (and acting on) true views of moral reality. If a God who is utterly good and righteous exists, and he has revealed what true goodness is, then the one with a view of reality that is based only on human opinion cannot be morally equivalent to the one with the true view.

In short, the hidden premise is false and the argument as framed cannot get off the ground. What counts for moral excellence is not whether or not a person is a believer (both are believers, though in different possible realities) but whether a person's view is true and, of course, on whether that person lives a life consistent with that view.

Second, if the God believed in by Christians exists, the person with the true understanding of what God wants is not granted his status with God on the basis of his behavior but on the basis of the fundamental commitment of his heart. The thief on the cross, for example, had no opportunity to lead a *good* moral life. He knew he deserved to die; he knew Jesus did not. His salvation was predicated on his relationship to God, which in turn was predicated on his faith in Christ as the righteous one. He may not have been moral by human standards, but he was forgiven by God and accepted: "Today you shall be with me in Paradise" (Luke 23:43). The thief's "life" was surely not diminished.

Carl: First, you have clearly indicated that you subscribe to the only counterargument available to you, namely, that believers are always at a higher level of goodness than nonbelievers. Thus if a nonbeliever matches a believer in every behavioral respect, the fact that the nonbeliever acts without the expectation of any reward or the psychological buttressing of God's perceived approbation cuts no ice; the nonbeliever is still allegedly morally inferior.

As a moral atheist, I find this viewpoint offensive as well as illogical. The atheist gets along on his innate sense of what is right as opposed to the believer, who must seek, via prayer and faith, outside support (i.e., the "crutch") for his behavior. Moreover, implicit in your argument is the view that God will punish the atheist for failing to believe in him, irrespective of his exemplary behavior, indicating that God does not look kindly upon those who are independent of the "believer's crutch." If this is the case, God is not living up to his own standards of goodness as quoted from the Sermon on the Mount. Thus, even if an atheist loved his enemies and allowed himself to be cheated or used by others (standards few if any Christians attain) simply because he is innately a good person, God would presumably still not accept him. Stripped of all its sophistry, the "true view," as described by you, requires slavish, unquestioning belief in an egocentric God.

Moreover, when you claim that both Christians and atheists are believers, you perpetuate the pernicious canard that asserts an equivalent rigor in the worldview constructs of atheists and Christians. In fact, such equivalence does not exist. Atheists, like other animals, process sensory inputs from their physical environment and respond accordingly. The world-

view that emerges in the brains of atheists is solely grounded in
these physically derived sensory inputs (i.e., it is a naturalistic
worldview). Christians, on the other hand, incorporate primi-
tively based mystical elements, for which there is no physical evidence, as major components of their overall worldview.
Weaning ourselves away from this atavistic behavior is essential for continued cultural evolution.

Second, from the standpoint of a moral atheist, your second
objection reveals a major immoral tenet in Protestant Christianity. Thus, if an atheist lives an exemplary life and dies an
atheist, he presumably will be rejected by God. Conversely, if
a hardened criminal, who obviously rejected God throughout his life (else the "fundamental commitment of his heart"
would have engendered behavior as exemplary as the atheist's),
suddenly professes his heartfelt belief as he approaches death,
he will be welcomed into paradise. Clearly belief in God is
the essential criterion for acceptance, which doesn't speak well
for God, the egocentric potentate. Thus, if an atheist died un-
believing and subsequently found to his astonishment that he
indeed has a soul, what would be his eternal fate? A human
sense of decency raises the hope that God would have a large
enough capacity for understanding and forgiveness to say to
the atheist's spirit, "Look, I know you didn't believe in Me in
your mortal existence, but you were upfront about your views
and lived a life worthy of any true-believing Christian. You
made an honest mistake. The celestial gate is open." What I
have learned of God from you suggests, however, that the possibility of such a humane scenario is vanishingly small.

PART EIGHT

RATS AND HUMANS

Minds and Brains

Carl sent Jim a link to "Rat to Rat, Kindness Takes Hold" by Nicholas Bakalar from the *New York Times,* July 10, 2007. Bakalar reports that Swiss researchers found that rats can develop "genuine reciprocity—that is, they [the rats in the experiment] were generous even with an unknown partner because another rat had just been generous to them." Claudia Rutte, a behavioral ecologist at the University of Bern, however, cautioned "against drawing conclusions about humans from work with rats." Still, there is published research "showing that humans act the same way."

This article set Carl and Jim on the issue of bodies and minds, things and ideas.

35

Rat to Rat, Kindness Takes Hold

Dear Carl:

Thanks for the link to the *Times!*

Rats may develop what looks like kindness to human beings who know what kindness is—a heartfelt mental attitude—but I doubt that they know they are being kind. They are simply acting on the impulse of such mechanisms that either promote or do not seriously impair the survival of the species.

The issue is how it is that we recognize such activity as kindly? Kindliness itself is a lot more than a mechanism, though it may well be linked with one. Surely, whether you see our nature as matter only, you must recognize that there is at least a difference between matter itself and the concept of matter or actions that look kindly and the actual attitude in the heart and mind of the rat. There is at least that sort of matter/idea dualism, isn't there? Well, I suppose not, not if you follow the arguments of the Churchlands and, I think, Dennett.[1] But let's not get into that. Dualisms of several types are still alive and well in modern philosophy.

Jim

---

[1] See the work of philosophers Paul and Patricia Churchland, who argue for *eliminative materialism,* and also that of philosopher Daniel Dennett and evolutionary biologist Richard Dawkins. On the dualist side of the argument, see the work of Nobel Prize winner Sir John Eccles, who speaks of *dualist-interactionism,* and C. S. Lewis, who rejects the "nothing buttery" of philosophical naturalism (or *physicalism*).

36

Chimps Too Are Kind

Dear Jim:

I've seen accounts of chimps taking care of a physically handi-
capped member of their group; a gorilla removing an irritat-
ing particle from the eye of another; a gorilla picking up a boy,
injured by a fall into its zoo habitat and gently carrying him to
the keeper's entry door; two elephants, reunited after twenty
years' separation, rushing together with great trumpeting and
lovingly intertwining their trunks. Your second sentence is
exactly on the mark. It is also the basis for human kindliness.
The fact that we can conceptualize kindliness relates to the
greater complexity of our brains. The unfortunate byproduct
of this enhanced complexity is our ability to conceptualize
our own death; hence the advent of religion.

Man, dualism just ain't! There's no evidence for it. Thinking about it doesn't bring it into existence.

Carl

37

Show Me Kindness

Dear Carl:

Show me kindness. Or any idea. Or a mind. I need it so I can
observe and thus learn about it.

Jim

38

Minds Emerge from Brains

Dear Jim:

You can read virtually limitless info on what happens to such concepts as kindliness, ideas and mind when the brain is altered. No one has ever been able to dissociate mind from brain. These are inescapable observations. The only reasonable conclusion is that the mind is an emergent property of the brain's complexity.

Less complex brains in nonhuman animals generate less complex thoughts. Damaged human brains can utterly change the personality and cognitive ability of an afflicted individual, even to the extent that he becomes as a lower animal, without a vestige of the conceptual capacity that you insist on spiritualizing.

Damaged brains, damaged minds

What happens to this person's "ghost"? Your "challenge" reveals the weakness of your worldview. You base it on the fact that the mechanisms by which thought is generated in the brain have not yet been worked out. It's the classic "God of the gaps" position. As more is learned, your challenge will gradually be met, and you will either be bereft or retreat to another gap, which in turn will be filled by more knowledge. And the gaps will keep getting smaller and smaller and smaller . . .

Cheers to the homunculus in your pineal gland!

Carl

39

Dualism Is Not Dead

Dear Carl:

Of course, you are right about the connection between mind and matter. Change the brain state and you change the consciousness—or eliminate it. We agree on that.

I am not divorcing mind from matter in the sense demanded by your critique. What I am doing is asking you to show me how they are the same or how one is a function of the other. There is enough difference between a brain state and an idea that brain state just neither describes nor fits what we recognize as an idea.

Science is not philosophy
You respond with the typical response of a scientist rather than a philosopher. You say, Just wait; what we can't explain today, we'll explain tomorrow. Really? How do you know? Despite the gradual and sometimes sudden new insights science gives us, it's always an act of faith to believe as you do. (You are the one with faith here.) The fact that neither you nor science in general has found a way to observe ideas is my evidence. Maybe science can't find a way. I'd like to see some data that fits the empiricist model.

There is some reason for your faith, of course. I don't deny that. But there is plenty of reason for my skepticism (look who's the doubter now!).

Moreover, philosophers have, from the earliest days to the present, found lots of ways to talk about ideas. We are doing so now. So it involves a dualism. So dualists have not been able yet to show how the two realms fit together. That means that they are in the same boat as the monists. There are some things that aren't yet known.

This not a god-of-the-gaps argument. Rather, it assumes

that there is plenty of evidence that reality consists of what we call *matter;* I believe that matter is sufficiently different from what we call *idea* to require some sort of dualism. We can and do use ideas all the time. They are required to help us deal with matter. I don't believe reality is only idea; but I do think that idea is so important that without it we would understand nothing—including matter.

Not a god of the gaps

I'd be happy to see the gaps in our knowledge filled. It's true there is a gap here. Consciousness has been the theme of a host of books and articles since the 1990s. I've read a few of them. But there is certainly no consensus among the philosophers. That science has ruled out any form of dualism is the result of a method that is limited to material-only explanations. It's okay to do that. But, then, don't take the methods of science as the only way to acquire knowledge of reality, especially that form of reality that seems so different from matter.

Jim

40

Subtle Distinctions

Dear Jim:
You're getting too subtle for me. You seem to acknowledge the dependence of the state of the mind on the state of the brain; then you want me to show you how one is a function of the other. Haven't you just agreed that the mind is a function of the brain? If you agree to this, then you accept the pure physicality of the process. If you contend that the brain is some kind of conduit for a supernatural agent, then you have to wonder why such an agent is so ineffectual as to be stymied

by injured brains or brains that differ intrinsically in their capacities to process information. Could the supernatural entities themselves have different levels of competence? Really, I think dualism gets into trouble here.

Experience   My "typical response of a scientist" is based on experience; "irreducible complexity" has invariably yielded to continued investigation. I don't see that viewpoint as an act of faith, but rather as an observation of how the scientific method has worked and continues to work. It's ironic that religious folks are so skeptical of the findings of empiricists (whose methodology is also based on skepticism about their own findings) but don't support the empiricists' approach of continued investigation, because it may lead to conclusions incompatible with religious dogma. Instead, they flee to the Bible, about which they have no skepticism whatsoever. Empiricists, on the other hand, willingly live with the knowledge that their conclusions are always subject to falsification via continual examination. Which position best fosters intellectual growth?

Changes in neuro-chemistry   But getting back to your evidence for duality—how is it possible to visualize an idea? Well, I hope we agree that it is a product of brain activity consequent to the processing of information previously entered into the brain. Some brains generate more and better ideas than other brains, and damaged brains (or those devoid of information, as in newborns) may be unable to generate any ideas. So it is reasonable to conclude that an idea in the brain has a physical existence characterized by changes in neurochemistry. The brilliant biophysicist with whom I'm going to have lunch tomorrow has a brain vastly more capable than mine with respect to the storage of information and the interplay of this information in a manner that generates new patterns. Ideas spew out of him like the high-pressure stream from a fire hose. If you asserted to him that the origin of his capacity was in any way supernatural . . . well, I wouldn't want to be there.

Okay, if an idea is a physical process when it's inside the brain, what happens when it leaves the brain and enters the environment via the spoken or written word? Can it be seen or contained or somehow still characterized as a physical entity?

This issue reminds me of a lovely "naturalist" gesture by my eldest daughter, Suzanne, at her college graduation ceremony. As she was receiving her diploma from the college president, she handed him a pinwheel and said, "This will help you to see the wind." I didn't know she intended to do this, but thought it was very moving, as did the president, who sent us a note later, indicating that he had mounted the pinwheel on his back porch, where it spun merrily in the breeze. **Of wind and pinwheels**

The point of this illustration is that, although we can (I hope) agree that the wind is a natural-world manifestation, i.e., a purely physical process caused by the nonuniformity of atmospheric temperature and pressure, we cannot see it except with respect to its effects on pinwheels, dust, clouds, etc. The same can be said for gravity and magnetism; both are manifestations of the physical properties of matter (I doubt that you would invoke the play of supernatural forces here), but neither can be directly observed. Like the wind, they are made apparent only through their effects on material objects. Clearly, ideas fall into this same category. They are physical manifestations of brain activity and are "visualized" by the effects they produce on other material objects, namely humans. In none of these instances is the invocation of duality required.

Yours, in faith that the sun will appear in the east tomorrow morning,

Carl

PART NINE

THE SOURCE OF OUR
DEEPEST DIFFERENCES

Though Carl and Jim had agreed to take a break from their dialogue, during the next few weeks, neither could keep completely silent. Essays by others and web links to still others were exchanged. Christopher Hitchens, Richard Dawkins, René Descartes, the goddess Athena, Cornelia Dean, Alister McGrath, Michael Gerson and even Plato tried to enter the stage but were booted off before they could steal the show. The course of Carl's and Jim's arguments could easily have been sidetracked. But discipline held, and when they returned to their posts, their minds were set on topics that served, not to bring about agreement, but certainly to advance their understanding of each other.

Carl first raises the question of what systems Jim and he would have affirmed if they had lived in ancient Greece. That question only inched the argument forward. Then an essay Jim sent to Carl set in motion a sustained dialogue. In "Christopher Hitchens, Man of Faith," Charles Strohmer, a Visiting Fellow at the Center for Public Justice in Washington, D.C., argues vigorously that atheism rests as much on faith as does Christianity.[1] Jim

---

[1] See <www.charlesstrohmer.com/wisdomproject.html>.

holds such a view; Carl does not. So, after Carl contemplates ending the conversation, the dialogue continues with an analysis of the deep divide between Carl and Jim: on what contrasting foundations do their commitments—Carl's atheism and Jim's Christianity—rest?

41

A Change of Focus

Dear Jim:

We got back [from Pennsylvania] yesterday, so my regular email address is again operational. I hope we'll be here for a while, but we may be called back to PA at any time in view of Nancy's mom's precarious health.

Anyhow, while I was driving back, I mulled over the history of our exchanges and have come to the conclusion that we've reached a dead end. I think we can agree that we're both stalwart representatives of our respective worldviews, but other than that we are now simply engaged in a useless war of words.

The only fruitful course of action I can envision is to try to understand why our attitudes toward religion are so different. If you want to engage in that way, let me know; otherwise, as far as I'm concerned, our discourse has concluded. It's been fun, though.

I hope Rich is okay.

Carl

42

A Way Forward

Carl:

Glad you're back safely. That's always a concern.

We haven't heard from Rich this past week, so we suppose that his health has not worsened. He's got a ways to go before he really is as healthy as he was before this terrible bout with strep gone wild.

About our dialogue. I was about to suggest something very much as you have done. We have made some progress in stating our own views but little in moving toward similar commitments. So at least for the moment, let's lay aside comments on the rationality or irrationality of Christian beliefs—that's been the topic of the past ten or so emails.

I do think, however, that we might make some headway if we were to discuss what each of us takes to be the most reasonable way to achieve knowledge. You emphasize human reason in general and science in particular; I emphasize the role that pretheoretical commitment (call it faith if you will) plays in both reason and the methodologies of science, especially in matters that science seems to me to be unable to address very well.

There is a second way I think we could make some headway. I would be willing to lay aside basing my own discourse on a commitment to the existence of God and simply examine your views from the standpoint of, if you will, my own unaided reason. After all, that's how the dialogue began weeks ago: I challenged your notion that ethics could be properly derived from purely naturalistic sources. I'd like to reexamine that one and ask you about other matters as well.

Nonetheless, I'm rather tied up at the moment with trying to conceive another book for IVP. So I would like to wait a few weeks before returning to the fray. We need time to cool our engines anyway.

Jim

43

Carl and Jim in Ancient Greece

As the debate developed, Carl raised an interesting question about what sorts of belief both of them might have had had they lived in ancient Greece. His final comment would seem to close off further conversation. Obviously, that didn't happen.

Carl: Just for fun, please Google "Parthenon Greece," click on the first entry, and read about this magnificent temple, as well as the characteristics of the great Goddess Athena (a quite superlative entity, I must say), for whom it was built.

    Given the awe-inspiring nature of the Greek culture, with the capacity to build such edifices, and their obviously profound and sophisticated religiosity, expressed in such magnificence, would you have been a part of that Greek religious community? Do you think you would have been debating nihilistic, hedonistic, naturalistic nonbelievers like me? According to Plato, atheists existed then as well. What I'm trying to get at is whether we differ intrinsically in our capacity for religiosity, irrespective of the nature of the religion at issue. [By the way,] I think I would have been an atheist then as well.

    I also think you and all the people whose views you find congenial would have vigorously defended faith in Athena against the onslaught of atheists like me, using the same arguments you use today in defense of Christian mythology. Addressing this issue is important because it helps to determine if the propensity for belief or nonbelief is independent of the object of worship.

    Jim: Carl, this is another one of those questions that requires utter speculation, speculation based on some notions that just couldn't be true. The project requires us to believe that you and I could be you and I in any meaningful sense.

An atheist in ancient Greece

An Athenian in ancient Greece

We couldn't. We are shaped by nature and nurture. Neither of us could be the same nature (we are children of specific parents; our DNA could not be the same). Our nurture would have been different, so different that we would not be us even if our DNA were the same. So I simply can't answer your question.

But I can speculate on what philosophically would have to be true for the question to make sense. It seems to me to imply that both of us have been so shaped by nature and nurture that neither of us was ever free to conclude differently about God, humans and the universe than we have concluded. If this is so, then we are nothing but robots, trapped by our DNA and our nurture.

Couldn't we have done other than we did, come to believe other than we do? You changed your mind a lot [over the early years of your life], if I recall your earlier emails. I did not so much change as develop. Could I not have changed? I certainly was under the influence of atheists at the University of Nebraska—notably my anthropology teacher. He told me, and I quote, "Sire, you read lots of books but they are all the wrong kind."

Why didn't I pick up on this, check into it further and change my mind? I did read lots of naturalist texts. Did I have no control? Was I not free to be an agent; was I only a reactor to natural and cultural stimuli? If so, I can't justly be held responsible for anything I do. If I steal, it's my genes and my upbringing. If I act like a saint, it's my genes and my upbringing.

I'm sure you don't believe that, do you? It reduces us to robots.

The implications of naturalism   But, then, if we are only material, there are only material causes—whether matter or cultural (all culture being composed of what is ultimately material or explained by matter). So maybe you do believe that you would be an atheist and I would be a religious Athenian because neither of us could be other than we are made to be.

But (and by the way), there were many belief choices in ancient Athens. The apostle Paul said to the philosophers in Athens (he explicitly mentioned Stoics and Epicureans) that the Athenians were so religious that they had a statue to an "unknown God." Intelligent, curious Athenians could have held a variety of beliefs, including being "god fearers" (Greeks with a Jewish belief) at any time from 500 B.C. to Paul's time and beyond. Were all of them captured by their nature and nurture?

More importantly, what in naturalism allows for genuine agency (freedom to choose freely from within one's own character and pondering)? And, to raise the issue with which our dialogue began, what is the naturalist's explanation for what must be assumed by any court of law that claims to be just—that is, that there is a difference between doing good (preserving life) and doing evil (taking life) that is more than the dominant human opinion that gives legal power to the court? To wit, is there really any difference between good and evil? All human beings certainly act as if there is. Naturalism doesn't account for this.

Carl: Alas, we are revisiting old issues. Yes, we are indeed "robots" in the sense that we are purely physical beings. As you have read, the "ghost in the machine," required to sustain religion, has virtually disappeared as a result of scientific inquiry. This issue and all the others raised in your above comments have been addressed in our prior correspondence. In any case, with respect to the basis for our different worldviews, I have my answer. We have said all we can to each other. I have really enjoyed these exchanges with you and look forward to our continued friendship.

Jim: Actually, there is at least one (I think there are others) Christian philosopher (Nancey Murphy) who is a monist with regard to the issues we are addressing, but she tries to show

how this is really the biblical view.[2]

Note that the Hebrew people were and often still are very oriented to the Land—not lines on a map but the very dirt of Israel. Even resurrection of the body points out the value of material reality. In Jesus' time the Greeks, especially the Platonists and Gnostics, thought the idea was nonsense because only the spirit (or Idea) was finally real. Christians have plenty of place (and reason) for a high view of the value of material reality and thus of a scientific method that takes it seriously. In fact, science arose within the framework of the Christian worldview—not atheism, not Greek philosophy, nor Hindu or Buddhist pantheism, but the mixing and blending and sometimes conflict between the Hebrew respect for material reality and the Greek passion for abstract thinking.

I suppose I do not have to point out that the phrase "the ghost in the machine" is a clever name-calling shorthand for the sophisticated philosophic notion of mind-body dualism. I can assure that the issue is not dead in philosophy, nor is it likely to be in the near future. If you'd like a bibliography of the continuing dialogue, I'd have to work to get one for you, but I'll do it if you like. The reason it appears dead in science is because scientists have defined science as a totally naturalistic discipline, unwilling to accept anything as unnatural (no miracles, for example, even though many events looking very much like miracles have been witnessed—the resurrection of Jesus, for example). Well, science is not going to detect anything that it has preemptively ruled out already.

But maybe the mind (the human soul or human spirit) simply can't be understood by natural science. Maybe its nature is not solely natural (i.e., material). Mind (human soul or spirit)

---

[2]Jim wrote this as it stands but would now like to qualify his suggestion that Murphy is a monist in the normal sense of the term. She explains herself in common language in "Nature's God," an interview published in *Christian Century,* December 27, 2005, pp. 20-25.

may be more than a mere function of the body. If it is, don't expect science to be able either to find it or to understand it.

44

A Final Colloquy   On Faith and Reason

After a cooling-off period when Jim and Carl took a break from a constant volley of emails, Jim opened the following long colloquy with what he takes to be the main distinction between his and Carl's basic starting points.

Jim: Yes, I suppose it is time for me to return to our dialogue. And I think it's a good idea to begin with the issue you raise in a recent email. It goes to the heart of our different approaches. Here is my understanding:

> Reason (with no faith and a lot of doubt) is primary (Carl).
> Faith (with a lot of reason) is primary (Jim).

Carl: That's not at all how I frame it. You have to try to understand the scientific method. What is primary is observation. A set of observations can give rise to a hypothesis, which attempts to explain them. This hypothesis is continually subjected to skeptical scrutiny and doubt. Additional observations are made that may strengthen, weaken or completely falsify the hypothesis. If, despite many attempts by myriad scientists, a particular hypothesis resists falsification, it becomes a theory.

Theories are not immune from doubt; they are still under constant scrutiny and are subject to modification as new information is acquired, although it is unlikely (but not impossible) that they will be entirely falsified, since they did pass their "undergraduate" tests as hypotheses. In this context,

Observation not reason— the methodology of science

doubt, skepticism and continual reexamination are positive attributes, essential for the acquisition of new knowledge.

Reason is *not* primary; it is the handmaiden of observation. This relationship is amply demonstrated by observing how chimps and other primates learn to use tools—first the observation, then the reasoning. Pure "reasoning" (i.e., brain circuitry running wild when not anchored by observation) leads into "Am I awake or dreaming when I write this?" A scaffolding of reason can also be built on faulty or inadequate observations, such as, a black cat crossed my path and five minutes later I broke my arm, so black cats are bad luck, or, I saw a bright light and heard a commanding voice, so God spoke to me. (Paul perhaps?)

Astrologers have battened on the credulity of those willing to accept a pattern of reasoning that is internally consistent but based on specious observations. Likewise, the origin of Mormonism might be subjected to a similar critical evaluation. It's interesting that Hitchens's debunking of Mormonism in his book is overlooked in the frenzy to attack his atheism. Do you think that the angel Moroni appeared to Joseph Smith with the Book of Mormon inscribed on silver plates? If not, why not? Millions of Mormons do and have constructed a formidable pattern of internally consistent reasoning based on this "miracle." Can the same be said of all the thousands of religions (perhaps I should say "scandals of the particular") that have emerged at various times down through the ages?

Clarifying terms: reason and observation

Jim: In the present discourse, not only have I misunderstood how you distinguish between reason and observation, you have misunderstood what I mean by "reason." I would never define reason or even "pure reason" as "brain circuitry running wild when not anchored by observation," never, ever!

It's interesting, though, that mathematics seems to use such "pure reasoning" without the consequence you suggest: its leading to "Am I awake when I write this?"

But it's my fault for not explaining that by "reasoning" I mean all the thoughtful brain activity associated with discovering the truth about reality. In other words, I meant "reason" to include (1) the recognition and identification of the empirical factors (i.e., the data accessed by observation; the act of accessing that data by the mind); (2) the more abstract reasoning that has to take place in the construction of hypotheses; and (3) the mental activity that is involved in testing the hypotheses. Reason, as I intended the term to mean, then, is not separated from observation but uses the results of observation to suggest what the data means.

Hypothesis formation

Your notion that "a set of observations can give rise to a hypothesis" is an instance of Lockean epistemology (sense impressions give rise to ideas or carry their own inevitable interpretation). This is a very dubious notion, one not held by philosophers of science such as Thomas Kuhn. (See *The Structure of Scientific Revolutions,* in which one of the conclusions is that every fact is theory-laden, roughly meaning that one doesn't know what a fact is until it has been associated with an idea. Shifting paradigms—intellectual constructs—control the identification and the meaning of a fact.)

Hypothesis formation is, I think, little understood, for what is happening is that a new explanatory model or overall master interpretation is being formulated. It may reflect the influence of suggestion of other hypotheses; it may come more or less out of the blue to the former of the hypothesis; it may be skewed, leaving out some of the data; it may be quite wrong. It may be more accurate to say that hypotheses—both ones that hold up under testing and those that don't—involve the imagination more than that they are triggered by the data itself. The empiricist model does not, I think, fit the reality of theoretical science as it is actually done. It may, however, fit what Kuhn calls "normal science"—the science that takes an already formulated paradigm and works out its implications for the understanding of new sets of data. Most science is normal science.

If you haven't read Kuhn's book and some of the responses by scientists and other philosophers, I think you'll find it a great read. When it was published in 1962, it was received as a challenge to the whole notion of how scientists have accomplished the amazing revolutions that have taken place in the few hundred years. The second and revised edition (1970) adds a postscript: Kuhn's response to his critics as well as a record of further development of his thought. There is also a 1996 edition, but I haven't read it.

In other words, I can say yes to almost all the description you give of the scientific method, though, of course, the scientific methods do vary with the object of the science. The life sciences are somewhat different from physics, for example. With this modification, is not your position that "reason (with . . . a lot of doubt) is primary"?

Still, some of the things you say, I would put differently. For example, you say that, in the scientific method, observation is primary. I would think that what is primary is, first of all, (1) the human selection of what is to be examined and thus what is to be observed, (2) an initial assumption of what sorts of things might count as data relevant to the explanation (this is necessary so that you can have some idea when what you see is what you are actually looking for, though the notion of what you are looking for may change as you gather what you think is data and find that it is not quite what you thought at first; observation and interpretation go hand in hand). For this "reason," I would say not that "reason . . . is the handmaiden of observation," but that they are equal partners.

Every search for meaning, every attempt to recognize what's going on, whether it's the existence and motion of the electrons or the question of God's existence, begins with assumptions that, strictly speaking, cannot be proven.

Assumptions necessary for living

On an individual level, every time I start to think, I believe I am awake. I do that now as I type. Am I? "Of course, I am!" I say to myself. Then, if I try to check on whether I am awake or not, I discover fairly easily that I can convince myself that I am awake. But if I ask what my evidence is for this conclusion, I find that I have done so by the very mind I am trying to check. I could therefore easily be misled. Last night—no kidding—I had a very vivid dream, a rather philosophic one. Even now I think that what I dreamed made a lot of sense. But maybe that's because I'm still dreaming and don't know it.

Don't you agree that any judgment you make that you are awake requires you to be awake in order for you to make that argument successfully? But what if you're not?

Now, do I go around worrying about whether my judgment that I'm awake is accurate? Of course not. I take it on what appears to me to be (1) reasonable evidence and (2) immediate consciousness that I am awake. So do most people, so it seems to me. But there could be reasons to doubt that I'm awake. I suppose this means it's dangerous to go overboard with doubt. But, then, how do we know we are going overboard? Funny thing, doubt.

What I am arguing here is that it is necessary (1) for there to be human epistemic equipment that functions to give us some truth about reality, (2) that we have that equipment and (3) that that equipment is functioning properly. It is usually easy for any of us to believe that all three of these are in place, especially when we are conscious and are seeking the truth. In fact, we believe this sort of thing most of the time. But it is not possible for us to be philosophically certain that this is the case. We could be wrong about any or all of our assumptions.

Every argument to prove any one of these premises requires all the premises to be true before we begin our argument.

In other words, our starting point as human beings seeking truth begins with a belief or commitment to the truth of these three premises, even though we cannot prove any one of them. This is simply the human condition. It is no different for a Christian or for an atheist. What we can do with our reason is reflect on the reasons we give ourselves for believing as we do. We can then evaluate these reasons and assess their "reasonability," but we will always be arguing in a circle. Many things (not just these three) will be assumed no matter where we begin. But there is a difference between how an atheist and a Christian can react to this situation.

From within the natural human frame, there is no way out of this circle. That is, there is no way for human reason to justify itself without trusting human reason to do so. Human reason must be autonomous; it must be necessary for a human being to determine on his or her own whether something is true or not. But autonomous human reasoning is caught in a circle. At this point naturalists have two choices: (1) to trust that human reason actually does access the truth whether this can be proven or not or (2) to become a complete skeptic and distrust every move the human mind makes.

In philosophy David Hume makes the first choice, especially with regard to the notion of *cause*. The notion that there is such a thing as cause cannot be proven, but we have to and do act as if it does exist. Nietzsche makes the second choice, saying, for example, that truth is a "mobile army of metaphors," there is no substance to claims to truth; these claims are like the images that have been worn off coins through time.

There is, however, a way out of the circle. If we human beings are made in the image of God, then it is reasonable to believe that we have been endowed with epistemic equipment not only adequate for our human functioning genera-

tion after generation but that this equipment can also lead us
to some truth about reality. Of course, that there is a God
and we are created in his image is a matter of faith. But it is a
belief that makes sense of our seeming ability to understand at
least some things about the nature of reality, both material (via
the methods of science) and spiritual (via special revelation—
Scripture, for example). Christian faith can be—and usually is
with thoughtful Christians—a reasonable faith. Christian faith
explains why human reason behaves as it does (even when it
makes mistakes); naturalism does not.

Christians and atheists are in the same epistemic situation.
Faith is required for both or either of them to place confidence in their views of reality—e.g., whether there is or is
not a God, whether science is the best way of understanding
the universe, themselves and their fellow human beings, etc.
Either or both of them could be wrong. Determining which is
right or whether some other view (say, pantheism) is right will
eventually require a faith commitment.

I conclude, therefore, that it is appropriate to ascribe faith
to nonbelievers as well as believers.

Carl: Let me take two different but complementary approaches in response to your above argument.

The foregoing is a beautiful illustration of the consequences of severing the brain's mental activity from its connection to the natural world. Even the most abstruse branch
of mathematics does not do this; it must trace its lineage back
to observations made in the world and attempts to understand
their significance. But your exposition calls into question the
validity of any observations obtained through the senses (with
which, strangely enough, you are equipped), asserting that
they cannot be proved.

First approach

Riding this train of thought out to the last stop must bring
you to the conclusion that the entire universe is a construct
of your consciousness. The natural world is an illusion; the

elements of it that come into being are strictly dictated by the direction of your attention. Anything you're not thinking about doesn't exist. Conversely, any aspect of art, literature, science, religion and the material universe (e.g., the solar system, stars, galaxies, etc.) becomes manifest if you direct your attention to it.

Of course all these constructs of your consciousness have no objective reality. God does not help you here. He is a construct, just like everything else; he even lacks the quasi-materiality of your quasi-physical surroundings. Now, what is the probability that this scenario is correct?

For example, as I write this attempt to critique your position, am I simply a construct of your consciousness? Are you arguing with yourself? Are my daily life, my interactions with my family and all my other activities constructs of your consciousness? For this to be the case, you would have to be thinking about me constantly because I don't perceive any breaks in my existence.

Moreover, you would have to know and be thinking about the lives of my children and grandchildren, with whom I interact frequently. The probability that you are maintaining my family and all its multifarious activities as constructs within your consciousness seems vanishingly small. Conversely, the probability that my family and I are objectively real and not simply constructs of your consciousness seems overwhelmingly high.

On the bases of these probabilities, your position falls to pieces and the entire natural world comes unequivocally into being. Likewise, if you pick up a rock, experience it with the senses that you cannot deny you possess and conclude that it is really a physical entity, you reestablish the connection between the natural world and your brain's mental activity and your arguments are overthrown. I leave the resolution of this issue to you, trusting that your intellectual honesty will prevail in any conclusion you reach.

Your argument is a beautiful exposition of the "brain in the jar" model. If you take a mature, fully functioning brain, place it in a jar, provide it with all necessary nutrients and isolate it from all external sources of information, you get pure "reason" of the ilk you have described above. Does this brain know whether it is awake or asleep? Does it know that it's in a jar? Does it know that it's a brain rather than some disembodied entity like God? If it's an intelligent brain, the fact that it's blocked from acquiring new information will force it into logic circles of the type you have described. Many Western philosophers were, in effect, "brains in jars," long on intelligence but short on information.

Second approach: brains in jars

It's interesting that Bertrand Russell described all their circular arguments in his *A History of Western Philosophy* but was not beguiled by them as you apparently have been. Maybe it's because he was an empiricist or (gasp) naturalist, and consequently open to new information. You no doubt remember reading the recent *New York Times* articles on evolution and the relationship between brain and mind.[3] Studies of the latter in particular are making it increasingly difficult for spiritually oriented people to hold on to the concept of a mind-brain duality, which is essential to your position.

Moreover, studies of evolution (also cited in the *Times*) are showing that human beings occupy no special place in the animal kingdom. Given such observations, reason can then come into play as an interpretive tool. What we can conclude is that man is an animal just like any other except for his more complex brain, itself a complete accident of evolution.

The more we learn, the more difficult it becomes to sustain a rationale for spirituality. Thus, it is abundantly clear that physically altering the brain can profoundly alter conscious-

[3] Cornelia Dean, "Science of the Soul? 'I Think Therefore I Am' Is Losing Force," *New York Times*, June 26, 2007, Science section.

ness, personality and every other attribute that you might associate with spirituality.

When you indulge in the type of discourse I'm responding to here, you're not using any observations, data or information that I can discern. Perhaps this is the essence of the spiritual point of view; observations and the acquisition of new knowledge are not necessary—in fact, they may be inimical to the maintenance of this viewpoint. In any case, what happens in the dissociation of mental activity from observation is a mental short-circuitry that in this day and age might be considered somewhat pathological.

Your argument that God provides an escape from this intellectual prison is not convincing. As implied in your argument, you have simply created him using the same type of unanchored "reasoning" with which you generated all the other aspects of your fanciful scenario. This leads to your ultimate oxymoron "reasonable faith." Your last sentence in the "God" paragraph is simply a bald, unsupported assertion at least half of which is incorrect. But you have made this assertion before and I have responded, so why beat a dead horse?

Response to the first approach

Jim: I don't hold anything like the pure subjective idealism you say follows from my understanding of the data of the senses! Nor does anything like this idealism actually follow from my views. (Relax. If I forget you, don't worry. You'll do quite well without me.) Moreover, I am already in print criticizing Descartes for making such a split between matter and idea that does, in fact, lead to something like you describe.

Hume held a very skeptical view of Lockean empiricism (the notion that data or facts suggest their own interpretation as they "write" on the blank slate of the mind). He was more skeptical of the data of such observation than I am. I am not at all radically skeptical. I believe that my epistemic equipment includes my ability to access through our senses a reality outside my mind. I do this because I trust the general reliability of our senses. Note, I *trust* (I have an implicit faith that in most instances we do gain genuine knowledge through our senses). But the sense of touch itself is not knowledge; our interpretation of it is (and that's a mental process).

We might possibly always *mis*understand the raw data of our senses (but, of course, generally we do not). And our senses themselves can be impaired; the blind can't see. But I can and do, at least with enough success to have lived long enough to propagate another generation that has propagated a further generation that hasn't yet propagated a fourth. See how fit I am, speaking Darwinianly, of course! Oh, and rocks fit nicely into my hand, but I try not to throw them.

In short, your first approach assails a position I do not hold and thus misses the mark.

Response to the second approach

As in your first approach, Carl, your second approach assumes that I have assumed the "brain in a jar" position. But I have done no such thing, as I hope I have made clear just above. You will find my own critique of the "brain in a jar" in my *Naming the Elephant,* though not by that name. By the way, when you say that my argument is "not convincing," the only thing that it can legitimately mean is "I am not convinced." That doesn't make the argument either weak or invalid, only unsuccessful in its present use.

Assumptions necessary for science

Now, let me continue my understanding of necessary assumptions, this time for science. [I reiterate that] for science, as well as for life in general, even to begin, it is necessary (1) for there to be human epistemic equipment that functions to give us some truth about reality, (2) that we have that equipment and (3) that that equipment is functioning properly. We cannot step out of the circle and test our testing equipment with other equipment known to be reliable. Rather, we have to assume that it is reliable enough to use at least to get started.

Trial and error (or often error and trial), we assume, will help justify or modify this method, but, then, even the reliability of that method can't be proven, strictly speaking. The whole process could be misguided. We don't think it is, but we can't prove it isn't. We accept its reliability by a faith that becomes backed by the results from our acceptance of the reliability of our epistemic equipment. If what we get "works" to consistently (a rational category) explain (a rational category) what we would like explained, our faith is justified. Faith in the reliability of our epistemic equipment is not proven, but it can be justified by observation correctly interpreted or thought to be highly probable of being correctly interpreted. Where there is the possibility of doubt, there must also be the possibility of faith. Both are present in the scientific method.

**Doubt or
curiosity**   *Carl:* As I indicated above, doubt is the stimulus for the continual reexamination and refinement of our understanding of the natural world. But it must be tied to observation. Through all our discussions to date, I am unable to discern how doubt and faith are compatible in your view. In fact, from your comments, I don't think you're at all comfortable with doubt. Moreover, I fail to see a connection between revelation and reason. I understand that you can construct a scaffolding of reason based on a "miraculous" occurrence (as has been done for all religions), but I am constitutionally unable to do that and am revolted by the prospect. I'm trying to understand why that's the case for me but not for you.

Jim: I would have thought that it is *curiosity* that is the stimulus for your (and science's in general) "continual reexamination and refinement of our understanding of the natural world." Curiosity (a desire for knowledge where knowledge is missing) is a positive motivation; doubt is only negative. Doubt can certainly be a secondary stimulus, but if it is the only stimulus, there would be no reason to proceed. You would just leave yourself in doubt. But, of course, you do not do that.

Revelation is how we come to get the vast bulk of our information. We trust the various media (to a degree) to tell us that there is a city in Mauritania named Tichît (I just looked it up in a Rand McNally atlas, which I believe I have reason to put my faith in when it comes to listing the cities in a foreign country). Almost all our knowledge of the world outside our immediate environment comes from revelation of one kind or another.

Revelation as a source of knowledge

Religious revelation is no different. If a Mormon tells me that he got his notion that God has a body, just as does the resurrected Jesus, from Joseph Smith's vision, I can use my reason (observation and abstract thinking) to see how reliable that vision is likely to be (not very, both you and I would say). The same approach can and should be used to check the reliability of biblical revelation. (There is, for example, a vast amount of evidence for the existence of Jesus and reason to think that at least the basic account of his life on Earth as written in the Gospels is historically reliable.)

The reliability of his testimony to the existence and character of God and to his own divinity is far harder to check, but it does not need to be taken on blind faith. If you doubt this, I point you to a large library of such scholarship (pro and con), much of which I both own and have read.

I don't think that the two of us are on opposite sides with regard to reason and revelation. Any time you accept a scientific account of some experiment or the justification for some scientific theory in an area you have not personally been involved in, you are basing your belief on revelation (with or without adequate justification). Of course, you trust some sources more than others, and you undoubtedly have reason to do this. But I, too, have reason to trust some sources more than others. We both trust (I think) Rand McNally and a great deal of scientific lore to which we have been exposed, yet we probably disagree on which of a number of other sources is more likely to be reliable. We both agree that the Book of Mormon is not reliable history; we probably disagree on whether the Gospels are in the same category. But we believe what we believe for the same "methodological" reasons.

Carl: You raise a very interesting issue. If we encounter something (an observation, an argument or some other inducement) that forces us out of the pattern of thinking that defines each of us, how traumatic would that be? Would it be necessarily bad?

For example, when Christian evangelists go about their sacred task, do they worry about the psychological impact they are having on their targets? Should they? Perhaps they feel like midwives facilitating the birth of a new Christian, a painful process followed by joy. Might this be presumptuous? Perhaps they are causing irreparable psychological damage to some people exposed to their blandishments. Should they shrug that off?

Closer to home, should each of us worry about psychologically damaging the other during the course of these discussions, or feel psychologically threatened ourselves? In my case, I feel challenged and stimulated, but not threatened, and I seriously doubt that I have the intellectual horsepower to convert you to atheism by force of argument. In fact, your "side" has the easier task because, as a "doubting Thomas," I could, like him, be persuaded by concrete evidence. I don't know what happened to Thomas, but I don't think he was cast into the outer darkness.

Anyhow, my side has nothing to offer you but the simple assertion that it feels good to throw off the shackles of superstition—a rather pallid alternative. So you definitely have the edge.

Jim: I take your point in the questions you raise about the trauma caused by evangelists. But if their "evangel" (their good news) is a hard word about them (that they are still in a profoundly broken relationship with a holy God) and if God has provided a way of reconciliation, then trauma may not be possible to avoid. Some solutions come only through pain.

Want to know what happened to Thomas, who doubted? See John 20:19-25 for reasons for the disciples' belief and Thomas's doubt and the following verses, 26-28, for what convinced Thomas and verse 29 for Jesus' teaching for those who did not and would not have the privileged direct evidence given the disciples. Then verses 30-31 give the Gospel writer's reason for recording the events that he's recorded. Follow the Gospel writer's advice in 31, and you will find where evidence lies (the sort of documentary evidence that leads historians to their probable conclusions).[4] All the Gospels are indeed written to explain and to give evidence for what is to be believed by those who want to know the truth about God, human be-

---

[4]John 20:19-31 reads as follows in the New Revised Standard Bible:

> When it was evening on that day, the first day of the week, and the doors of the house where the disciples had met were locked for fear of the Jews, Jesus came and stood among them and said, "Peace be with you." After he said this, he showed them his hands and his side. Then the disciples rejoiced when they saw the Lord. Jesus said to them again, "Peace be with you. As the Father has sent me, so I send you." When he had said this, he breathed on them and said to them, "Receive the Holy Spirit. If you forgive the sins of any, they are forgiven them; if you retain the sins of any, they are retained."
>
> But Thomas (who was called the Twin), one of the twelve, was not with them when Jesus came. So the other disciples told him. "We have seen the Lord." But he said to them, "Unless I see the mark of the nails in his hands, and put my finger in the mark of the nails and my hand in his side, I will not believe."
>
> A week later his disciples were again in the house, and Thomas was with them. Although the doors were shut, Jesus came and stood among them and said, "Peace be with you." Then he said to Thomas, "Put your finger here and see my hands. Reach out your hand and put it in my side. Do not doubt but believe." Thomas answered him, "My Lord and my God!" Jesus said to him, "Have you believed because you have seen me? Blessed are those who have not seen and yet have come to believe."
>
> Now Jesus did many other signs in the presence of his disciples, which are not written in this book. But these are written so that you may come to believe that Jesus is the Messiah, the Son of God, and that through believing you may have life in his name.

ings and the world we live in.

Faith and reason in tandem

Of course, all this evidence is subject to critical analysis. And it has received a huge amount from those who have become convinced Christians, those who remain unsure and agnostic, and those who are atheists. In every case, evidence and abstract reason (not, of course, what you call "pure reason") work together with faith, whether that faith is trust in our own reason unaided by God (Carl) or trust in our own reason because it has been made in the image of God's reason (Jim). Faith and reason can be at odds but do not have to be so. Thinking Christians—and yes, there are millions of them—strive to keep them from being at odds when they really aren't. Indeed there is "reasonable faith."

While I was thinking about how I would answer your email, I was also reading Alister McGrath's *Dawkins' God*. McGrath quotes Anglican theologian W. H. Griffiths-Thomas, one-time principal of Wycliffe Hall, Oxford:

> [Faith] commences with the conviction of the mind based on adequate evidence; it continues in the confidence of the heart or emotions based on conviction, and is crowned in the consent of the will, by means of which the convictions and confidence are expressed in conduct.[5]

This seems a lot like the attitude you have when you attempt by the scientific method to frame, modify and improve your worldview, your overall take on life.

---

[5] W. H. Griffith-Thomas, quoted by Alister McGrath, *Dawkins' God: Genes, Memes, and the Meaning of Life* (Malden, Mass.: Blackwell Publishing, 2005), p. 86.

WINDING DOWN

At this point Carl and Jim agreed to end their attempts to inform and to change each other's brain (Carl) or mind (Jim). But some emails continued, mostly as notes to pass on to each other articles that relate to the issues they addressed in the correspondence published here.

A couple of these late emails addressed the topic that opened their dialogue. Carl and Jim suggest readers take this as a mild resolution to that key topic of morality—mild because the resolution was basically a decision to agree to disagree.

45

Enough Is Enough

Dear Jim:

A final comment on morality.

Everyone does what feels right at the time, i.e., what each of us does at any given moment depends on our physical nature at that moment. Our physical nature at that moment is a product of our genetic heritage and the environment to which we have been exposed up to that moment. That's the way my brain works with respect to evaluating human behavior.

If humans are to survive, people whose behavior is inimical to that survival will naturally be controlled by those whose behavior fosters human survival. If that doesn't happen, humanity will die out. That's my concept of morality. Rival claims with respect to what is good will be adjudicated by natural selection.

Are you sure you want to continue these exchanges? I'm sure what I've said is as alien to you as what you've said is to me. When you talk about nonmaterial ways of understanding reality, we might as well be in different universes. As I've said before, I would be interested in understanding the basis for our profoundly different worldviews (although I think I already do—it's a difference in brain chemistry—unless my homunculus is on permanent leave), but we seem just to get right back into the same old verbal warfare.

Carl

46

Sure Is!

Dear Carl:

What you have just written is precisely what I have tried to get you to admit to. To wit, that there is only power—in this case the power of being able to stay alive long enough to keep the species going. I agree with you. It means that morality will be adjudicated by the winners. If that's what you mean by morality, then I have nothing more to say.[1]

Wrong and right no longer have a meaning that is universal enough to sustain a pluralist society. Humanity's pluralist lifetime on earth will be cut short not by global warming but by its inability to sustain itself. Totalitarianism or extinction: those will be the options. And neither of them will be any worse than the other, for better and worse have passed away as a category.[2]

---

[1] It was only as I was reviewing these emails that I recognized that Carl had made this assertion repeatedly in the conversation. For example, "We can articulate the notion that it's better to exist than not exist, but this sentiment is simply a distillation of the survival mechanism present in all living organisms. Without this mechanism, life would be impossible. So the ascribing of significance to the human preference for existence is pointless" (no. 9).

[2] Carl disputes this bleak assessment of his worldview. The argument that recourse to spiritualism is required for moral behavior is disproved by *observations* of nonbelievers' behavior as well as that of nonhuman primates and other social animals. Carl sees no reason to suppose that religiosity has any greater power to sustain humanity than the biologically reflexive urge to preserve life.

Afterword

Carl's Comments

In the body of this work I was simply reacting to Jim's religious assertions, translating "Naah!" into some semblance of a rational, though often over-heated, response. Now I am enjoined to generate a coda to this exchange from my standpoint and try, using Jim as an exemplar, to be civil in the bargain. This is a tall order for me.

First, I want to affirm that all of my remarks in our dialogue are unedited initial reactions to Jim's arguments; no post hoc syntactical or logical cosmetic surgery was performed. I believe this is the case for Jim as well. You, dear readers, in effect have eavesdropped on what our friend Phil calls our freshman dorm bull session.

My second affirmation is the acknowledgment of profound respect and affection for Jim, the embodiment of warmth, humor, dignity and intellectual honesty. Some might ascribe Jim's exemplary character to his Christian persuasion; I do not. In this respect he resembles many atheists whom I have the honor to call my friends.

Wracking brains and changing minds. So, what's the basis for the apparently unbridgeable gulf between the worldviews that Jim and I hold? I've wracked my brain for an answer and find that the conventions of language as exemplified in the very expression I've just used ("I've wracked my brain") may hold the key. This expression (connoting an extraphysical "self" that uses the body) manifests the concept of mind-body dualism that is the keystone of religion.

Similarly, the word *mind* is linguistically utilitarian; it summarizes the

workings of the brain, but it also carries the connotation of an extraphysical entity that works through the brain. Combining these linguistic elements in the expression "I've changed my mind" virtually eliminates the
physical aspect of the duality, opening the door to all that heaven allows.
From our discourse, I conclude that Jim is among the population that has
taken this path.

Evidence closes the celestial door. Some of the religious among you may
be angered, others saddened or nonplussed by my refusal to follow in Jim's
footsteps. The reason for this refusal, reiterating the argument I made in
our discourse, is the overwhelming preponderance of evidence against the
existence of mind-body dualism. Thus, any alteration in the physical nature of the brain (stroke, Alzheimer's disease, psychoactive drugs, surgical
intervention, etc.) changes its functional capacity and consequently the
"mind" that it expresses. If, as amply demonstrated, the mind is purely a
manifestation of brain function, then the concept of an extraphysical component of the human persona must be abandoned and the celestial door
must close.

(For the nonbeliever, then, the linguistic connotations of "I've changed
my mind" can be brought down to earth. The expression can be considered a more efficient way of saying, "This brain has received new inputs,
and upon processing them has become reconfigured.")

Functional and dysfunctional brains. Therefore, my explanation of the
divergence in the worldviews that Jim and I hold is that key structural and
functional elements of our brains differ, consequent to dissimilarities in
our genetic heritage and early formative experiences. In the proven absence of any extraphysical contribution to brain function, I can't see how
a reasoned analysis can lead to any other conclusion. In other words, the
"Carl brain" is not architecturally or neurochemically constituted to entertain the notion that it harbors a spirit. This is not to denigrate the fantasti-
cal thinking of which the complex human brain is capable and which can
be the fountainhead of great art, music and literature. However, brains in
which such thinking assumes disproportionate importance (to the extent
that it supplants thought grounded in the senses) are to varying degrees
dysfunctional.

Doing what comes naturally. Extending the purely physical worldview, I contend that Jim is an inherently good person and would remain so as an atheist. Likewise, I can assert that my atheistic worldview has not burdened me with uniquely negative personal attributes, as can be verified by my friends, as well as my beloved wife, children and grandchildren. Like Jim, I do what feels right in a given situation. He wouldn't admit it, but this is biologically reflexive behavior for both of us; no spiritual entity plays a role in this process.

Our common humanity. Finally, we should acknowledge that, for all our differences, Jim and I have major attributes in common. We love great art, literature and music, and we are awed by the beauty and grandeur of the universe. Jim may be puzzled by the fact that a nonbeliever can share such sentiments, but this commonality can be readily explained as residing in the shared physical complexity of our human brains and the consequent emergence of such sophisticated appreciations, rather than as the result of spiritual input accessible only to believers. In this context, positive "humanoid" characteristics, including altruism, humor, compassion, fairness, love and artistic expression have been observed in nonhuman primates and other social animals, despite their evident lack of religious affiliation.

With respect to an appreciation of the wondrousness of our origins, reality does not take a back seat to mythology. Thus, to me the knowledge (based on modern observations, not ancient mythical accounts) that we are made of stardust and starlight and are manifestations of the evolving universe in all its immensity and diversity is infinitely more compelling than the purported actions of the anthropomorphic deity created by Christians trapped in the morass of magical thinking engendered by their dualist mindset.

Despite the profoundly dissimilar viewpoints of Christians and atheists, however, we must be mindful of the overarching concern that unites us all, namely the preservation of our precarious occupancy of this fragile, beautiful, "pale blue dot" that is our home. Whether we are Christians or atheists, we love our children and want them and their descendants to thrive. In view of the social nature of the human animal (i.e., our universal interdependence), this goal can be achieved only if biological and cultural diversity are preserved worldwide. Such diversity is what makes evolution and human life possible. So, given the glorious paradox of our divergent viewpoints and convergent interests, let us celebrate our common humanity and strive to foster its continuation. The afterlife will take care of itself.

Carl Peraino
September 8, 2008

Jim's Comments

Over seventy emails from April 14 to July 19, 2007, on topics ranging from the high moral character of brilliant scientists to the dull credulity of religious believers, from the veritable heavens of transcendent, spiritual reality to the lower region of utterly mechanistic materialism—and what was accomplished? Painfully little, if one looks for changed minds on either side of the atheist-Christian divide. But a great deal if one considers what the seemingly fruitless discourse shows about intelligent dialogue itself and about the intellectual subtlety of both atheism and Christianity.

I admit that I am the culprit who fired up this conversation and kept it burning despite the several times it sputtered and almost died. It did, of course, finally die or at least remain only as a few embers. But who knows when one of us will cast wood on those embers and the flames rise again?

Still, both of us, as can be seen, are supplying eulogies. This is mine.

Common commitments. Carl and I do not disagree on everything. In fact, our conversation is based on a common commitment to rational discourse. We both hold that there is a truth about the world and that the human mind is capable of finding some of it. I believe we have this capacity because we are made in the image of God. Even after the Fall, we retain some rational capability because of God's common grace. I believe that all our abilities are due to the Godlike nature in which we have been created and that God has revealed much of who he is and what constitutes the morally good and spiritually rich life. Carl also believes that the human mind is capable of discovering some truth about reality. But this has nothing to do with God. Rather, a purely natural process of evolution, while not itself designed, has brought into existence human beings with such minds. For him the human mind is autonomous, that is, on its own. There is no source of information outside ourselves, no revelation from beyond.

Though to some extent both of us are skeptics, neither of us is post-modernist. Our skepticism is bounded by our fundamental commitment to the existence of a reality that can be known, understood and spoken about with some degree of realism and accuracy.

Second, Carl and I agree on much of the content of moral character—honesty, truthfulness, industriousness and faithfulness to and care for our families, our local communities, the larger, worldwide human family and the environment. Both of us believe that atheists and Christians alike can live highly moral lives. Both of us wish to live this way ourselves, though I for one—and I think Carl too—am willing to admit I don't always live up to my own moral notions.

Common disagreements. Still our disagreements are substantial. I see moral character grounded in the supreme goodness of God; Carl sees it as a result of undesigned evolution, deriving from the survival of the fittest. In fact, our dialogue begins precisely on this point of disagreement; the disagreement is never resolved. For me, this is one of the great puzzles of our discourse. Why can't Carl see that explaining why we have moral notions is far from explaining what it means to have them. I say they need a foundation in something outside human opinion or human desire. He says no. Readers will have to decide which of us—or neither—has got this right. I think it will be important for them to do so. The notion of a transcendent foundation for both morality and rationality is so central to Christian faith that without the one, we can scarcely have the other.

There are many other matters on which we disagree: (1) naturalistic, unintended evolution vs. some form of God's creative design; (2) science based on observation and not requiring faith vs. science and religion both requiring faith and reason; (3) the cultural peril of Christian belief vs. the cultural contribution of Christian faith; (4) the moral character of some animals vs. the merely seemingly moral character of these animals; (5) denial of any so-called signals of transcendence vs. the plethora of such signals in every segment of reality; (6) the highly questionable moral na-

ture of the biblical God vs. the character of God as the transcendent, righteous foundation for true morality; (7) the necessity for God (if he/she/it
were to exist) to be dipolar vs. the lack of such a necessity and a denial of
its reality; (8) the cultural danger of any firmly held belief vs. the cultural
danger of some firmly held false beliefs; (9) mind and body as one vs. mind
and body in some form of complex duality.

As I reexamined our emails for the purpose of publication, I found
some dangling conversations, some elements of each other's arguments we
missed or ignored. But most of these are inconsequential and the rest must
continue to dangle or perhaps be picked up again later.

Sufficient reason for changing one's mind? These obvious lacunae and
omissions raise a deeper question: Do either of our arguments constitute a
sufficient set of reasons for anyone else coming to believe what either of us
believes? Carl will have to answer for himself, but I have no hesitation.

For the necessary existence of a transcendent foundation for morality—
yes, I think my argument should persuade. For a difference between mind
and body—yes, again. Yes, too, for which is primary to the scientific quest,
doubt or curiosity. For the merely apparent moral character of animals—
yes. For its being unnecessary for any God who is the foundation for morality to be dipolar—yes.

But, taken as an argument for the truth of the Christian faith itself, my
argument is far from conclusive and, I should think, far from necessarily
persuasive. The very best argument for the Christian faith is barely cited.
Starting where I started, I could not see how to pull the dialogue into its
aura. And what is that argument? It is simply stated in one word—Jesus—
but it takes many words to unravel. (I only scratched the surface in emails
number 14, 31 and 44.) There were barriers preventing my developing this
line of argument, and they were not removed by my arguments.

Why good arguments often fail. One principle is clearly illustrated by
our arguments: often arguments—though they are thought good by their
proponents—still fail to persuade, especially when the issues are the basic
ones of life. That leads me to the final question of this afterword: Why do
Carl's and my arguments largely fail to convince each other?

It is one thing to find that our *bad arguments* fail. They should, and some of both Carl's and my arguments are bad. At least once we both mis-understood what each other means by *reason* and *faith* (no. 44). And Carl often imagined I believed things I didn't believe. So these arguments had to fail.

The tough question, however, is this: Why do our *good arguments* often fail? This is a question Carl should answer as well. For surely he believes his arguments are good, does he not? Why did I not believe they were good and accept them? I think that some of the reasons for both us are the same but some—especially one—is very different.

First, some good arguments (those based on true premises and contain-ing no formal fallacies) are too complex for one of the parties to under-stand. That does not seem to me to apply to our dialogue. I don't even want to admit that it might. Well, okay, I admit that it might apply to either of us, but I don't think it does.

Worldview commitments. Second, some good arguments are not seen to be based on true premises. The biggest reason for this is that every premise is rooted in a commitment to a particular worldview—naturalism, theism, deism, etc. (nos. 6, 7). When Carl says he is tethered to "natural-world" logic (nos. 9, 16), he means that he will accept no notion that involves the possibility of something "nonnatural," that is, supernatural or transcen-dent. When I respond that I'm tethered to ordinary, traditional Christian theism (no. 17), we have set our poles in the ground of our different fun-damental mental orientations. If neither of us will accept any notion that contradicts (or perhaps even threatens) our worldview, neither of us will find our opponent's argument convincing.

Carl, in fact, makes a point of this when he quotes the Oxford don who fails to see even a hint of intelligent design in the universe (no. 31): "Look," he said, "I'd better lay my cards on the table; I'm an atheist." Carl simply adds, "Me too."

Moral failure. Third, some good arguments, if convincing to one who previously disagreed, demand major changes in orientation and behavior. They are costly.

If I were to become an atheist, I would have to abandon my long-held Christian faith. My whole reason for living would change. I would stop all my religious disciplines and lose the close camaraderie of my fellow believers. What would I become? Carl asked. I said a hedonistic nihilist (no. 31), probably behaving as humanly moral as I had before but finally in some sort of existential despair. I would feel lost in space, tipsy, utterly disoriented.

If Carl were finally to agree that the Christian God actually exists, he would have not only to acknowledge this but also to change his pattern of life. He might not have to change much of his moral behavior, but his reason for living would change, and he would have to worship God. At present, this is just about the last thing he would want to do; he would consider it throwing his brain and his moral sense out the window. I think he would rather rail against such a God and even express hatred at the notion of his existence. Such changes for both of us would be very costly. Are either of us willing to pay the price?

Long ago Augustine recognized the profound psychological/moral/intellectual perversion that is involved in coming to hate the truth: "Why does truth call forth hatred?" Augustine asked. Then he answered:

> Simply because truth is loved in such a way that those who love some other thing want it to be the truth, and precisely because they do not wish to be deceived, are unwilling to be convinced that they are indeed being deceived. Thus they hate the truth for the sake of that other thing which they love, because they take it for the truth. They love truth when it enlightens them, they hate it when it accuses them.[1]

Is this one of the reasons for Carl's intransigence? Or mine? There is no way for me to know about Carl. For myself, I say no. It is, however, a possibility for both of us.

Still, atheists do become Christians (C. S. Lewis being one of the most noted) and Christians (or at least people who once understood themselves to be Christians) do become atheists (Carl, I think, would count himself among them).[2]

---

[1] Augustine *Confessions* 10.23.
[2] See *God and the Philosophers: The Reconciliation of Faith and Reason*, ed. Thomas V. Morris

Spiritual blindness. Finally, there is an even more serious possibility. Carl, of course, will have no place in his worldview for this explanation. It can only be true if the Christian faith in general (or something very like it) is true. So Carl cannot possibly agree with what I am about to say. But if the Christian worldview is, in fact, true, then this explanation is at least possible.

The apostle Paul had perhaps the strongest statement of the syndrome:

> What can be known about God is plain to them [humankind], because God has shown it to them. Ever since the creation of the world his eternal power and divine nature, invisible though they are, have been understood and seen through the things he has made. So they are without excuse, for though they knew God, they did not honor him as God or give thanks to him, but they became futile in their thinking, and their senseless minds were darkened. (Romans 1:19-21)

What Paul says in the text that follows only strengthens his case against those who deny God's existence. What, then, is the malady he identifies? Spiritual blindness is the usual term applied.

Is it appropriate for me to raise this possibility in this form at this time? I did not do so in our emails. I believe, however, that to fail to raise the issue now would do no justice to the Christian faith nor to the God whom, if he exists, we should all acknowledge and worship.

If such a God does not exist, then the dire warning of the consequences of his existence is a mere illusion worthy of being dispensed by a wave of the hand. But, if such a God does in fact exist—and that is what our discourse has been all about—then the dire implications of his existence are a part of the argument. They are where, to use a cliché, the rubber meets the road.

Carl notes that Pascal's wager is a paltry scare tactic and unworthy of any God.[3] Okay, I don't think it's a very good argument either. But what I

(New York: Oxford University Press, 1994); and Kelly James Clark, *Philosophers Who Believe: The Spiritual Journeys of Eleven Leading Thinkers* (Downers Grove, Ill.: InterVarsity Press, 1993).

[3]Blaise Pascal, *Pensées*, trans. A. J. Krailsheimer (Harmondsworth: Penguin, 1966), no. 418 (233), pp. 149-53.

do think is that it has one extremely important value. It shows us what the stakes are. If the Christian God exists and we miss him, we miss not only the very essence of reality but face a rather unhappy future.

Spiritual sight. In the final analysis, from a Christian point of view, all discernment of truth—whether it is the true conclusions from a good argument or simply the immediate or intuitive recognition of some truth—is prompted by the Spirit of truth, that is, by the Holy Spirit. If our epistemic equipment is not cleansed from the corruption of our sin, we will never see the truth. But this is especially true of matters relating to belief in God and his presence in our lives. The apostle John wrote, "By this we know that he [Jesus Christ] abides in us, by the Spirit that he has given to us" (1 John 3:24).

Such a requirement may seem an insuperable barrier. It might look like only those arbitrarily chosen by God will come to know the truth about God. But God is gracious. Anyone who seriously seeks to know him can do so. "Ask, and it will be given you," Jesus said, "search, and you will find; knock, and the door will be opened for you" (Matthew 7:7). With an open-minded, open-hearted search, a prayer for God to open one's eyes to his reality, then with an encounter with Jesus Christ in the Gospels, anyone can be on his or her way to knowing not only that God exists but that he will profoundly reward those who diligently seek him (see Hebrews 11:6).

This is not enough. I do not wish to end here. There is so much more to say about the spiritual nature of our ability to know.[4] But Carl and I have agreed to let our emails stand as they are. Enough is enough. So this brief teaser will have to do.

Nor do I wish my dialogue with Carl to shipwreck on the shores of an unintended insult to his integrity. So I trust that Carl, and readers who largely agree with him, take my hard, unhappy words not as an arrogant

---

[4]"Man's real difficulty is that he is spiritually blind: the truth of God does not impress the sinful mind for what it is. . . . The remedy consists in the restoration of spiritual vision and sight, of the opening of ears and eyes resulting in an intuition of the truth of God. . . . [When the restoration has occurred:] The total inward man now *sees* revelation as revelation; he *intuits* truth as truth; he *hears* Scripture as the truth of God. . . . The result of this intuition is *plērophoria*—spiritual certainty" (Bernard Ramm, *The Witness of the Spirit* [Grand Rapids: Eerdmans, 1960], pp. 84-85).

reliance on my own judgment but rather as a natural consequence of what I understand to be the truth about reality. It's a view that requires all of us to yield our own judgment to the bar of truth and the God of truth, justice and mercy.

God save all of us from our fumbling minds and erring hearts!

James W. Sire
September 8, 2008

Study Guide

One of the important characteristics of *Deepest Differences* is that it does not *imitate* a dialogue. It *is* a dialogue. The intellectual positions Carl and Jim hold, defend and criticize are here displayed as they were generated. As a consequence, a number of specific issues surface and are discussed, then disappear only to reappear in a different context sometimes with significant variations or qualifications. This study guide is designed to help sort out the ideas that are keys to the overall argument. To use it fully, therefore, readers will need to move back and forth throughout the dialogue, picking up clues from one section, adding them to clues from later sections and then evaluating their import and coming to their own conclusions.

In general the following sections focus on one or a few key ideas in the order they first appear in the dialogue itself.

Morality (nos. 1—7, 10, 35—36)

1. How do Carl and Jim differ in their conceptions of morality? Is morality an absolute that can exist in a prebiotic universe or is it a concept that applies only to vulnerable living beings? Can an invulnerable God be moral? What reasons do Jim and Carl give for their disagreement on this issue?

2. Can undirected evolution, with its emphasis on the survival of the fittest, give rise to moral behavior, that is, to behavior that can be evaluated as right and wrong? Do you think survival itself is a value? Why or why not?

3. If you subscribe to God-directed evolution, do you think it proceeds via a different mechanism than undirected evolution, thereby eliminating the negative connotations of the "survival of the fittest" concept? How would God-directed evolution differ from human-directed evolution as it is practiced in animal and plant breeding? Does the latter activity also incorporate the "survival of the fittest" concept?

4. Jim thinks that morality requires a transcendent foundation, that is, a foundation that undergirds all correct human judgments and finds all incorrect human judgments wrong. Carl eschews transcendence and thinks moral behavior (i.e., behavior that promotes survival) is a product of natural selection. With whom do you agree and why?

5. Why does Jim think that there is a difference between *morality* as such and the *sense of morality*? What does Carl think? Why?

6. How would you explain the possibility of morality in the sort of world you think exists—a world with God or a world without God?

Theology (nos. 10—15, 31, 32)

At the heart of their deepest differences lie two fundamental ideas: (1) the existence or nonexistence of God, and (2) should God actually exist, what his characteristics would probably or necessarily include. This topic is in the background of the entire book, so the answers to many of the following questions will involve the content of many of the emails.

1. With respect to God, what does Carl mean by *monopolar* and *dipolar*? Why does Carl think that God, if he were to exist, would necessarily have to be dipolar? Why does Jim disagree? What do you think?

2. Summarize Jim's understanding of who God is. What is the main source of his understanding?

3. How does Carl describe what he takes to be Jim's God? What charges does he make with regard to God's character?

4. How does Jim respond to each of Carl's charges?

5. The problem of evil (Why, if God is both good and omnipotent, has he created a world that has had and continues to have such a surfeit of human suffering?) is a major issue for theists. In what way does Carl raise the issue? How does Jim respond? What role does Jim say free will plays? How does Carl respond to the concept of free will?

6. Carl suggests that nonbelievers who are (overtly) equally as moral as believers are advantaged because they do not require a religious crutch to aid them in achieving moral parity. Jim counters that believers are subject to a higher standard of morality and, if they actually live by that, are morally superior to nonbelievers. With whom do you agree and why?

7. What does Carl mean when he says "our [his and Jim's] brains are wired differently"? How does this notion relate to Carl's denial that God exists? Why does Jim reject Carl's notion of different brain wiring? What do you think about this issue?

8. What case can be made for God and/or Jesus being insane? Why is this question more than an exercise in name-calling?

For further reflection on this question, Jim recommends C. S. Lewis's *Mere Christianity*. Carl recommends Elizabeth Anderson's "If God Is Dead, Is Everything Permitted?" in *The Portable Atheist: Essential Reading for the Nonbeliever* and *Philosophers Without Gods: Meditations on Atheism and the Secular Life*.

9. Jim charges Carl with speculating about what God, if he exists, would be like. Why does he do this? Why is Jim so hesitant to consider either Carl's or his own speculation? What role do you think speculation should play in determining what God is like or whether he exists?

10. Carl speculates about what God could "get out of creation." On what is that speculation based? On what is Jim's speculative response based? How valuable do you think such speculation is to an understanding of (1) the basis for people's belief in God or lack thereof and (2) the basis for the determination of whether God exists or not?

11. Why does Jim readily assert the inscrutability of God? Why does Carl reject the notion of God's inscrutability? With whom do you agree?

12. Summarize Carl's reasons for not believing that any god exists. Summarize Jim's reasons for believing that the God of the Bible exists. Where do you stand on this issue? What reasons can you give for your current judgment or, if you are not very sure, your current opinion?

Evolution (nos. 15—18, 32)

1. How does Carl understand the notion of intelligent design? Why does he think it is not a science? What objection does Jim have to Carl's understanding?

2. Why does Carl emphasize the importance of the Dover trial? Why does Jim discount its value in determining the character and viability of ID as a scientific theory? Are the proponents of ID justified in classifying it as a scientific theory? What criteria must ID meet to be so classified?

You may wish to consult the following accounts and critiques of ID and the Dover trial before finishing your own evaluation. Carl recommends the books by Francisco Ayala, Kenneth Miller, Robert Pennock and Neil Shubin. Jim recommends the books by William Dembski and "Dover in Review" by John West (see "Relevant Readings").

3. Summarize Carl's understanding of the role of evolution in the origin of human beings. Why does Jim not take a firm position with regard to the issue of evolution and the origin of human beings?

4. What is the key issue that makes the nature and the development of the biosphere important to the question of whether God exists? Have you, like Carl, reached your own conclusion on this issue, convinced that no god was involved in the origin of the universe or its evolutionary development? Or are you more like Jim, convinced that God is the Creator of the universe but unsure of the role a God-designed evolution might have played? Why?

"Relevant Readings" lists many books on the relationship between evolutionary theory and Christianity. Carl especially recommends David Quammen's *The Reluctant Mr. Darwin*, Robert Pennock's *Intelligent Design Creationism and Its Critics* and Carl Sagan's *Varieties of Scientific Experience*. Jim recommends Francis Collins's *The Language of God*, William Dembski's *The Design Revolution*, and Benjamin Wiker and Jonathan Witt's *A Meaningful World*.

5. How do Jim and Carl, respectively, see themselves in relation to other animals? What is your position and why?

6. Carl and Jim differ in their personal assessment of how prevalent atheism is among scientists. Who turns out to be correct? What is Carl's view of why so many elite scientists are atheists? Is his conclusion justified? Why or why not? How important are these statistics to a responsible answer to the question of God's existence?

Christianity and violence (nos. 27, 30)

1. According to Carl, how are God, Christian history and violence linked? Do you agree that Jim's attitude is smug? Why or why not? Jim insists on differentiating between what Christianity teaches and how self-confessed Christians behave, whereas Carl disallows such a distinction. With whom do you agree and why? For some reason Jim did not respond to Carl's accusation that Christianity merits no claim to superiority over other religions with respect to the inculcation of violence. How would you respond?

For further discussion of this frequent charge against Christian faith, Carl recommends Elizabeth Anderson's "If God Is Dead, Is Everything Permitted?" in *Philosophers Without Gods* and *The Portable Atheist*. Jim recommends John W. Wenham's, *The Enigma of Evil*, and Alister McGrath's, *The Dawkins Delusion?*

Minds and brains (nos. 35—40)

1. Is the mind a purely physical manifestation of brain activity, or is it a

separate, nonphysical entity that acts through the brain? What is the evidence for each of these possibilities?

2. How central is the foregoing question to the issue of the existence of God?

For further information on this topic, Carl recommends Gary Lynch and Richard Granger's *Big Brain* and Robert Burton's *On Being Certain*. Jim recommends Paul Copan's *How Do You Know You're Not Wrong?*

Reason, faith and science (nos. 3, 10, 44)

The issues of reason, faith and science are complicated and vexing. From the beginning of history, they have been a staple subject of philosophy, theology and science. The authors know that the disagreements on them will not be laid to rest by their dialogue. Here are questions to help readers recognize and come to terms with some of the twists and turns the arguments take.

1. How do Jim and Carl (each separately) define the following terms: *reason, pure reason, faith, observation, scientific method?*

2. What is the relationship between faith and reason? What is Carl's view? What is Jim's view? Which view do you think is the most accurate and helpful? Or do you have an alternate view? What is it?

3. What does Jim mean by *reasonable faith?* Why does Carl reject this notion? What do you think?

4. Why does Jim think science—and actually all knowledge—is based on faith? Why does Carl disagree? What do you think?

5. According to Jim, what is revelation and how does it play a role in our coming to know anything—scientific, secular or religious?

Doubt, science and religion (nos. 24—27)

1. What view of doubt does Doctorow's Rabbi Sarah Blumenthal commend? Why?

2. What sort of religious conviction does Blumenthal advocate? What is her understanding of God? Why does she find it encouraging?

3. According to Carl, how is certitude linked to violence? Why? Why does Jim disagree?

4. According to Carl, how is doubt linked to the scientific method? What would Jim put in the place of doubt as more valuable for scientific pursuit?

5. What role, if any, do you give doubt as a positive factor in coming to a proper understanding of any issues we may confront, such as God's existence, ourselves, others and our interaction with the natural world?

To help answer these questions Carl recommends Robert Burton's *On Being Certain*. Jim recommends his own book *Habits of the Mind*.

Reason and rhetoric

1. Describe the rhetorical styles of Carl and Jim. What sorts of language or jargon does each use? Who is more direct and easier to understand? How does each respond to the other's criticism? Does their rhetoric affect the effectiveness of their arguments? How and why, or why not?

2. Do you think that the temperaments displayed by Carl and Jim affect the character or the persuasive power of their arguments? How and why?

3. Both Carl and Jim explain why they think their own "good" arguments do not persuade the other. What are those explanations? Which explanations seem the most likely to you? Are there other explanations? If so, identify them.

4. Do biographical factors help explain the disparate positions that Jim and Carl hold? How or why not?

Deepest differences

1. The deepest differences between Carl and Jim, as they themselves

admit, lie in their very different worldviews. What are those world-views?

To answer this question in detail, examine the entire text and consider how Carl and Jim would respond to the following questions. The brief possible answers given below only give hints as to the specific ways in which Carl or Jim—or anyone else—answers these questions.

2. What is the foundation of reality: a personal God (theism), an impersonal God (deism), the physical cosmos itself (naturalism) or a cosmos that is ultimately divine (pantheism)?

3. What is the nature of external reality: a designed creation (theism; deism), matter or matter and energy in a complex but ultimately rational relationship (naturalism), an illusion (pantheism)?

4. What is a human being: a person made in the image of God (theism), an independent personal creation of God (deism), a highly complex but totally physical being with personal characteristics (naturalism), a spark of the divine (pantheism)?

5. What happens to a person at death: resurrection to life with or without God (Christian theism), not clear (deism), extinction of personal existence (naturalism), reincarnation (pantheism)?

6. How can anyone know anything at all: by being made in the image of an all-knowing God (theism), through innate human reason given by God (deism), human reason alone (naturalism), human knowledge is limited, relative and ultimately illusory (pantheism)?

7. How can a person tell the difference between right and wrong: by being made in the image of God who is goodness himself (theism), through innate human reason given by God (deism), through the application of autonomous human reason (naturalism), right and wrong are relative and illusory (pantheism)?

8. What is the meaning of the human sojourn on earth: to fulfill God's ultimate purpose for humankind, the establishment of the kingdom of

God (Christian theism), to establish and promote human flourishing on earth (deism), to promote human flourishing as understood solely by the autonomy of human reason (naturalism), to proceed through endless cycles of emanation from ultimate reality and returns to ultimate reality (pantheism)?

For a fuller explanation and evaluation of worldviews, Jim recommends his book *The Universe Next Door,* 4th edition. Carl recommends Carl Sagan's *Varieties of Scientific Experience: A Personal Search for the Existence of God.*

9. Which worldview, Carl's or Jim's or one of the others listed, gives the best explanation of your experience and understanding of this world and your own life?

Relevant Readings

Aikman, David. *The Delusion of Disbelief.* Carol Stream, Ill.: Salt River, 2008.

Anderson, Elizabeth. "If God Is Dead, Is Everything Permitted?" In *Philosophers Without Gods,* edited by Louise Antony. New York: Oxford University Press, 2007.

Ayala, Francisco J., et al. *Science, Evolution and Creationism.* Washington, D.C.: National Academy of Science Press, 2008.

Bakalar, Nicholas. "Rat to Rat, Kindness Takes Hold." *New York Times,* July 10, 2007.

Berger, Peter. *A Rumor of Angels: Modern Society and the Recovery of the Supernatural.* New York: Doubleday, 1969.

Blomberg, Craig. *The Historical Reliability of the Gospels.* 2nd ed. Downers Grove, Ill.: InterVarsity Press, 2007.

Burton, Robert A. *On Being Certain: Believing You Are Right Even When You Are Not.* New York: St. Martin's Press, 2008.

Carroll, James. *Constantine's Sword: The Church and the Jews, A History.* Boston: Houghton Mifflin, 2001.

Collins, Francis. *The Language of God: A Scientist Presents Evidence for Belief.* New York: Free Press, 2006.

Copan, Paul. *How Do You Know You're Not Wrong? Responding to Objections That Leave Christians Speechless.* Grand Rapids: Baker Books, 2005.

Dawkins, Richard. *The God Delusion.* Boston: Houghton Mifflin, 2008.

Dembski, William A. *The Design Revolution: Answering the Toughest Questions About Intelligent Design.* Downers Grove, Ill.: InterVarsity Press, 2004.

Dembski, William A., and Michael Ruse. *Debating Design: From Darwin to DNA*. New York: Cambridge University Press, 2004.

DeWolf, David, et al. *Traipsing into Evolution: Intelligent Design and the Kitzmiller vs. Dover Decision*. Seattle: Discovery Institute Press, 2006.

Gould, Stephen Jay. *Wonderful Life: The Burgess Shale and the Nature of History*. New York: Norton, 1989.

Harris, Sam. *Letter to a Christian Nation*. New York: Knopf, 2006.

Hitchens, Christopher. *God Is Not Great: How Religion Poisons Everything*. New York: Twelve Books, 2007.

————, ed. *The Portable Atheist: Essential Readings for the Nonbeliever*. New York: Da Capo Press, 2007.

Johnson, George. "Free-for-All on Science and Religion." *New York Times*, November 20, 2006.

Jones, John E., III (Judge). "Memorandum Opinion in the United States District Court for the Middle District of Pennsylvania." *Tammy Kitzmiller, et al., v. Dover Area School District, et al.* Case 4:04-cv-02688-JEJ, Document 342, filed 12/20/2005. See <www.sigmaxi.org/resources/evolution/051220_kitzmiller_342.pdf>. For the entire set of trial documents see <http://en.wikipedia.org/wiki/Kitzmiller_v._Dover_Area_School_District_trial_documents#Trial_Materials>.

Jones, Preston, ed. *Is Belief in God Good, Bad or Irrelevant? A Professor and a Punk Rocker Discuss Science, Religion, Naturalism and Christianity*. Downers Grove, Ill.: InterVarsity Press, 2006.

Kluger, Jeffrey. "What Makes Us Moral." *Time*, December 3, 2007, pp. 54-60.

Krakovsky, Marina. "Chimps Show Altruistic Streak." *Discovery*, January 8, 2008, p. 63.

Kreeft, Peter, and Ronald K. Tacelli. *Handbook of Christian Apologetics*. Downers Grove, Ill.: InterVarsity Press, 1994.

Kuhn, Thomas S. *The Structure of Scientific Revolutions*. 3rd ed. Chicago: University of Chicago Press, 1996.

Lewis, C. S. *The Abolition of Man*. San Francisco: HarperSanFrancisco, 2001.

————. *Mere Christianity*. New York: Macmillan, 1952.

Lynch, Gary, and Richard Granger. *Big Brain: The Origins and Future of Human Intelligence.* New York: Palgrave Macmillan, 2008.

McGrath, Alister. *Dawkins' God: Genes, Memes, and the Meaning of Life.* Malden, Mass.: Blackwell Publishing, 2005.

————. *The Dawkins Delusion? Atheist Fundamentalism and the Denial of the Divine.* Downers Grove, Ill.: InterVarsity Press, 2007.

————. *Intellectuals Don't Need God and Other Modern Myths.* Grand Rapids: Zondervan, 1993.

Miller, Kenneth R. *Only a Theory: Evolution and the Battle for America's Soul.* New York: Penguin, 2008.

Moreland, J. P., and William Lane Craig. *Philosophical Foundations for a Christian Worldview.* Downers Grove, Ill.: InterVarsity Press, 2003.

Novak, Robert. "Remembering the Secular Age." *First Things,* June/July, 2007, pp. 35-40.

Oppenheimer, Mark. "The Turning of an Atheist." *New York Times Magazine,* November 4, 2007.

Pennock, Robert T., ed. *Intelligent Design Creationism and Its Critics: Philosophical, Theological and Scientific Perspectives.* Cambridge, Mass.: MIT Press, 2001.

Quammen, David. *The Reluctant Mr. Darwin: An Intimate Portrait of Charles Darwin and the Making of His Theory of Evolution.* New York: Atlas Books/Norton, 2006.

Ratzsch, Del. *Science and Its Limits: The Natural Sciences in Christian Perspective.* 2nd ed. Downers Grove, Ill.: InterVarsity Press, 2000.

Sagan, Carl. *Varieties of Scientific Experience: A Personal Search for the Existence of God.* New York: Penguin, 2006.

Shubin, Neil. *Your Inner Fish: A Journey into the 3.5 Billion Year History of the Human Body.* New York: Pantheon Press, 2008.

Sire, James W. *Habits of the Mind: Intellectual Life as a Christian Calling.* Downers Grove, Ill.: InterVarsity Press, 2000.

————. *Naming the Elephant: Worldview as a Concept.* Downers Grove, Ill.: InterVarsity Press, 2004.

————. *The Universe Next Door: A Basic Worldview Catalog.* 4th ed. Downers Grove, Ill.: InterVarsity Press, 2004.

————. *Why Good Arguments Often Fail: Making a More Persuasive Case for Christ.* Downers Grove, Ill.: InterVarsity Press, 2006.

————. *Why Should Anyone Believe Anything at All?* Downers Grove, Ill.: InterVarsity Press, 1994.

Stenger, Victor J. *God: The Failed Hypothesis: How Science Shows That God Does Not Exist.* Amherst, N.Y.: Prometheus Books, 2007.

Wenham, John W. *The Enigma of Evil: Can We Believe in the Goodness of God?* Grand Rapids: Academie Books, 1985.

West, John G. "Dover in Review: A Review of Judge Jones' Decision in the Dover Intelligence Design Trial." Discovery Institute. January 6, 2006. <www.discovery.org/a/3135>.

Zimmer, Carl. *Evolution: The Triumph of an Idea.* New York: HarperPerennial, 2006.

Biographies

James W. Sire

Education
University of Nebraska, B.A., Chemistry and English, 1955
Washington State College (now University), M.A., English, 1958
University of Missouri, Ph.D., English, 1964

Professional Experience
Instructor in English, University of Missouri, 1958-64
Assistant Professor of English, Nebraska Wesleyan University, 1964-66
Associate Professor of English, Nebraska Wesleyan University, 1966-68
Associate Professor of English, Northern Illinois University, 1969-70
Adjunct and Visiting Professor, teaching worldview analysis in Philosophy
    and Theology departments at numerous universities and seminaries in
    North America and Europe
Editor (chief), InterVarsity Press, 1968-84
Senior Editor and Campus Lecturer for InterVarsity Press and InterVarsity
    Christian Fellowship, 1984-98

Academic Interests
English and world literature
Christian apologetics
Worldview research and analysis
Christianity and the academic disciplines

Membership in Professional Societies
Modern Language Association
American Scientific Affiliation

Publications

Fifteen books and many articles on worldviews, apologetics and the relationship between Christian faith and the academic disciplines, including:

The Universe Next Door (InterVarsity Press, 1976; 4th ed., 2004); trans. into 18 languages

The Discipleship of the Mind (InterVarsity Press, 1990)

Why Should Anyone Believe Anything at All? (InterVarsity Press, 1994)

Habits of the Mind (InterVarsity Press, 2000)

Václav Havel: Intellectual Conscience of International Politics (InterVarsity Press, 2001)

Naming the Elephant: Worldview as a Concept (InterVarsity Press, 2004)

Why Good Arguments Often Fail (InterVarsity Press, 2006)

A Little Primer on Humble Apologetics (InterVarsity Press, 2006)

Carl Peraino

Education

Lebanon Valley College, B.S., Chemistry, 1957
University of Wisconsin, M.S., Biochemistry, 1959
University of Wisconsin, Ph.D., Biochemistry, 1961

Professional Experience

Postdoctoral Fellow in Oncology, University of Wisconsin, 1961-64
Instructor in Oncology, University of Wisconsin, 1964–65
Assistant Biochemist, Argonne National Laboratory, 1965-70
Biochemist, Argonne National Laboratory, 1970-78
Senior Biochemist, Argonne National Laboratory, 1978-89

Research Interests

Mechanisms of hepatocarcinogenesis
Mechanism of enzyme regulation
Molecular properties of ornithine aminotransferase

Membership in Professional Societies

American Association for Cancer Research

Federation of American Societies for Experimental Biology (Biochemical Society)

Membership on National Committees

Chemical Pathology Study Section, National Cancer Institute, 1977-82

Editorial Board, *Cancer Research,* 1980-88

Award

University of Chicago Award for Distinguished Performance at Argonne National Laboratory, 1983

Publications

Author or coauthor of approximately one hundred research articles (accessible on the Internet), including "Reduction and Enhancement by Phenobarbital of Hepatocarcinogenesis Induced in the Rat by 2-Acetylaminofluorene," coauthored with R. J. Michael Fry and Everett Staffeldt, *Cancer Research,* 31 (October 1971): 1506-12. This paper signaled a significant shift forward in cancer research.

Index

This index lists all authors cited in the email exchange, footnote commentaries and afterwords. It also lists key ideas relevant to the main topics discussed. Such notions as *argument, God, reasons*, are almost ubiquitous and thus are not listed.